ITALIAN

PIZZA
and
Hearth Breads

ITALIAN
PIZZA
and
Hearth Breads

Written and illustrated by
ELIZABETH ROMER

Clarkson N. Potter, Inc./Publishers
DISTRIBUTED BY CROWN PUBLISHERS, INC., NEW YORK

Recipe for kneaded dough: Wash your hands and a bowl thoroughly. Pour meal into the bowl, add water gradually, and knead thoroughly. When it is well kneaded, roll it out and bake under a crock.

Cato 234-149 B.C.

In the artistic hands of a Neapolitan *pizzaiolo* the pizza becomes a divine food that besides satisfying the palate and the stomach, consoles the spirit, mind and eyes and infuses a pleasing and delightful warmth in the veins.

Guiseppe Porcaro 1985

Published in the United States by Clarkson N. Potter, Inc.,
225 Park Avenue South, New York, New York 10003

Originally published in Great Britain by Michael O'Mara
Books Limited, 20 Queen Anne Street, London W1N 9FB

CLARKSON N. POTTER, POTTER, and colophon are trademarks of
Clarkson N. Potter

Manufactured in Spain

Library of Congress Cataloging-in-Publication Data
Romer, Elizabeth.
Italian Pizza and Hearth Breads.

Bibliography: p.
Includes index.
1. Pizza   2. Bread   I. Title.
TX770.P58R66 1988   641.8'24   87-13823
ISBN 0-517-56693-1

10 9 8 7 6 5 4 3 2 1

First American Edition

CONTENTS

For my godson John Jerome O'Mara, with love.

Acknowledgments

Many people have helped me in the preparation of this book and first of all I would like to thank Vicky Hayward and Joanna Lorenz for their invaluable work of editing. My thanks are also due to Carolyn Hart of Clarkson N. Potter for her excellent advice. My friends John G. Ross and Linda Rhodes cheerfully accompanied me on trips to Naples and Genoa in search of pizza and Professor Hans Goedicke gave me many interesting insights into ancient Egyptian culinary history and also that of his beloved Austria. Adriano Chiarioni and Guiseppe Lombardi with great enthusiasm and kindness made the chapter on *The Italian Pizzeria* possible. I am also very grateful to Valentino Caldiero, Ciro Moffa, Imola Solfanelli, Mariella Morandi, Maddalena Beligni, Signora Cetraro, Silvana Cerotti and Silvana Caponnetto, who so charmingly takes charge of the grateful diners at Genoa's 'Le Fate' restaurant and who told me so much about her city and its cooking.

An especial thank you to my husband John Romer who allowed me to ruffle the serene shelves of his library, explored Naples with me and happily ate my *pizze*.

PREFACE

This book sets out a personal view of a small part of the great Italian culinary heritage. It is about the beloved pizza, emblem of the Neapolitan man in the street.

Pizza, a robust urban food originally sold by street traders to the numerous and poor Neapolitans who had no hearths or ovens to bake in, forms the main theme of the book. A second, allied theme, that of *schiacciata* or *focaccia*, explores the domestic hearthbreads prepared for hundreds of years by generations of country women at their own firesides. Last come the courtly *torte*, elegant tarts and pies made from fine pastry filled with delicate ingredients, which were lovingly made by mediaeval and Renaissance cooks to tempt the appetites of the well-to-do, and which today, in simpler form, still grace the tables of the Italians. The pizza, the hearthbread and the tart are but variations on a single theme, a disc of dough that by the cook's ingenuity has been brought alive with fillings and flavours.

This book will, I hope, give the reader a sense of the spirit and place of this extraordinary food, pizza, that in some form is as old as fire and corn, has been appreciated in poor city streets and royal palaces and has travelled from the old world to delight the new.

The recipes in the greater part of the book are for open pizza, called in Italy *pizza alla Napoletana*. I have arranged them in different sections according to the main ingredient in the seasoning, such as seafood, artichokes, onions or peppers. In each of these sections I have digressed to give a little information about the ingredients, in some cases the history, their uses in Italian cooking, and recipes for conserves to be made from them. Also, where it is necessary I have suggested substitutes. Where there are none I have tried to give a guiding principle as to why a particular ingredient is used. Does it provide a smooth base? Does it respond well to heat, or is it used to give a high note to the general flavour? With the basic reason for using a cheese or vegetable in mind you may then choose an alternative with similar properties, but always remembering the essential rule, that whatever ingredient you select, it must be of the freshest and best quality at your disposal.

At the side of each recipe there is a short list of ingredients so that you may flick through the pages and decide which recipe will match what you have in the larder and what, on the other hand, you may need to buy for a particular pizza. These ingredients lists are given in order of quantity not in order of appearance in the recipes.

I have also included a section on the oil, olives, herbs and spices that Italians use to embellish their pizza, and of course there is a chapter devoted to the heart of the pizza, the crust.

Many of the chapters begin with descriptions of people and places: Naples; Tuscan women who bake their own hearthbreads; Genoa, her markets, her famous cooks and their recipes. My good friend Adriano Chiarioni has taught me about baking pizza and the place that *pizzerie* have in Italian society today. This information and more given me by other friends in this pleasing business has gone into the chapter called 'The Italian Pizzeria'. These digressions are intended for those who like to browse, as I do, through cookery books and dream about and re-member the places where the recipes originated.

To stress the obvious, Italian food is made by Italians living in Italy. It is important to know about the people, their cities, the countryside from which the produce comes and the history of their cuisine, if we are to begin to understand why their dishes are as they are and why it is that we eagerly travel to countries like France and Italy to eat their food. Modern Italians are the product of centuries of civilisation of a very high order. The relationship between them, their food and their land has not yet been ruined by industrial revolution. They enjoy, appreciate and re-spect good food and they conserve with pride the regional differences in their cooking.

Elizabeth Romer
Aiola 1987

PROLOGUE

Imagine a hot summer night in Rome; a pizzeria set in a garden outside the city walls, its crowded tables placed under scented pine trees. The air is warm and filled with the sound of crickets. Vine-covered trellises shelter groups of friends who have left the hot city streets and driven into the countryside to eat a midnight pizza. The tables at which they sit are covered with faded cloths, they drink carafes of *vino rosso* out of plain glasses and waiters hurry from the kitchen to serve them, bearing dishes of searing-hot pizza fragrant with oregano, garlic and luscious tomato. And just what is the nature of this pizza, this pie, which is what the word pizza means, that they have come to eat? What place does it enjoy in the wide spectrum and long history of Italian food?

The story behind the pizza is far older than even the crumbling walls of ancient Rome. From anonymous Neolithic people to my present Tuscan neighbours, people have baked simple hearthbreads, *galettes* or *focacce* on hot stones, clay discs and, later, metal bakestones specially prepared for the purpose; and being pleased by variety they have seasoned them with whatever good things there were to hand. These simple breads are the forerunners of pizza.

To make a rough cake of bread Neolithic people first had to have grain. Wild wheats occurred spontaneously. Emmer, einkorn and barley grains sprang from the tree-sheltered soil of the Levantine coast, the hills of north-eastern Irak and most of Asia Minor, spreading themselves through this natural bread cradle of the western world. Once the Neolithic people had the grain they then needed the tools to harvest it.

Lying in a museum case in Jerusalem there is a tiny sickle, polished by the rasp of ancient corn. It seems to me touching, both in its delicate simplicity and its antiquity; a poignant thing. It was made by the people of the Jordan Valley, that near-Eastern nursery of mankind. Twelve thousand years ago they learnt how to fashion flint into microliths, take a bone or antler, arm it with these strong slim teeth and in the cool morning go out under cloudless skies with their tiny sickles and cut the wild corn. There is no way of naming the first person who tasted wild wheat, then crushed the grain, mixed it with water into a paste and baked it on a fire. All that may be said is that at certain times microliths and sickles were made, querns and grinders, pottery, bread moulds and ovens, and from this ancient worn paraphernalia we may assume that the making of bread evolved.

In Egypt near the looming 4th-Dynasty pyramid of Chephren there are other relics which to me are equal in fascination to the giant tombs; these relics are ovens that were used to make bread for the workers, ovens that are still red from the effect of their long-spent flames. From this era four thousand years ago you can count a dozen different sorts of bread, and later in the New Kingdom period *c. 1580-1069 B.C.* nearly forty varieties are named in lists of offerings in tombs and temples. But no recipes, as we know them, have yet been discovered written on papyrus rolls or carved into stone.

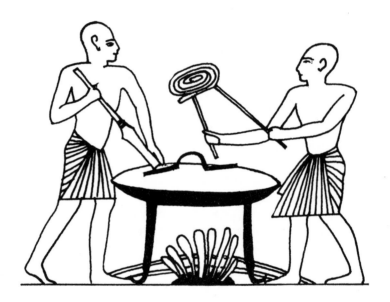

When working on our archaeological expedition in the Valley of the Kings at Egyptian Thebes, I would often go into the tomb of Ramesses III to look at the brilliant painted scenes of his palace. These include some of the best culinary scenes in Egyptian art. The Pharaoh's kitchens have shelves laden with fancy breads of many shapes and sizes and no doubt rare flavours. You can see pans of boiling oil held on trivets over leaping flames, and in the oil the cooks prepare twists of fried batters, coiling them with the aid of two batons. This scene reminds me of Cato's *encytum*, for which he gives a recipe in *De Re Rustica*, a work on the management of life in the country, many of whose instructions still hold good in modern Tuscany. In other ancient Egyptian tombs of different periods there are scenes of brewing and baking, with the dough being kneaded by foot in great jars – this habit led a puzzled but ever-observant Herodotus, a thousand years later, to exclaim 'Dough they knead with their feet, but they mix mud with their hands.' *Book II, 36.*

There are many fables told in cookery books about the discovery of yeast; tales of lazy Greek cooks throwing old dough into new dough with predictable results. These tales of 'instant discovery' are pretty fiction. The leavening effect of natural yeast must have occurred spontaneously long before the substance itself was named. Egyptian bread and beer were made in the same yeasty-atmosphered room. The beer brewed from bread baked slightly so that the yeast was not destroyed, then crumbled in water and left to ferment was then flavoured and strengthened with dates and strained before it was drunk. With the extra sugars from the fruit it must have been a potent brew. Analysis of the dried residue in pottery jars filled some four thousand years ago enabled chemists working in the 1920s to isolate a previously unknown and quite extinct yeast *Saccharomyces Winlockii*, named after the American archaeologist Herbert Winlock, who found the ancient jars at Thebes. Presumably the unleavened breads of the Bible, mixed in wooden bowls and baked on pierced clay discs, were the natural result of a process where speed was an important factor. Not so the breads produced in ancient Egyptian bakery/breweries where the relaxed continuous processes of baking and brewing must have led to natural yeasts hanging in the warm air, settling on brews and doughs alike in the mutual processes of rising and fermentation.

Sprouting grain held a profound religious significance for the ancient Egyptians. The bread and the beer that they made from the grain were seen as gifts of the gods. And as part of a pact made with their gods the Egyptians offered a proportion of the generous bounty of their fertile land at the altars of the great temples of the Nile Valley. A popular kind of ancient Egyptian bread shaped like a plump triangular cushion is still made in Upper Egypt, and this is what we ate when working at Thebes; our supply was baked in a mudbrick oven by Om Kalthoom, the wife of our expedition cook. The bread is called *aish shemsi*, sun bread, and it is leavened with sourdough and raised in the sun. Om Kalthoom's oven is not so different from those of the ancient Egyptian bakers.

In modern Egypt bread still has a sacred side to its nature as in ancient Egypt. It is considered to be a gift of God and to be treated with respect; none is wasted and if by chance a morsel should fall to the ground it is picked up with a murmured apology to the Almighty. And in modern

Tuscany very much the same ideas apply – olive oil and bread are sacred gifts and it is a grave sin to waste either of them. I have been told by Tuscan friends that I may add to my years in purgatory by the number of crumbs I have left by my plate. Pizza, too, is regarded by Neapolitans as possessing more significance then a simple everyday food.

However, the master bakers of the ancient world must surely have been the Mesopotamians, and from the records they have left we can even recognize something close to a modern seasoned *focaccia*. They had as many as three hundred varieties of bread. The simpler kinds they baked by clapping them on to the sides of heated pottery cylinders, and similar barrel-shaped ovens are still to be seen in North Africa and the Yemen today. But by the third millenium B.C. they had domed ovens in which they could bake leavened bread. These breads came in all manner of sizes and forms, from tiny table breads to large loaves, and the great variety was achieved by using different sorts of flours and flavourings of diverse herbs and spices. They used juniper, mint, cumin and coriander and, as today, garlic and onions were important ingredients. They mixed their doughs with sesame and olive oils, and other liquids such as beer, milk and a sort of butter. They may have also used some of their thirty varieties of cheese as enrichments. Sweet breads were made with fruit and honey. Tuscans make a similar sweetened bread today at grape harvest, with honey, black pepper and ripe grapes.

The Mesopotamian palace cooks would bake bread to amuse as well as to taste good. They used moulds to make shapes like hands, hearts, ears, heads and even plump round breasts. There is, in the Mesopotamian culinary records, all carefully impressed upon clay tablets and only recently translated, a complicated recipe for a rich stew of some variety of game bird which was served upon a flat bread seasoned with spices. After the bread had been specially cooked on a dish, like a pizza base on a baking tin, it was seasoned with spices, onion and garlic, covered with the meat and sent directly to the table. The bread under the stew was not, I think, intended as a trencher to hold the food; as anyone who has ever drawn potsherds on an archaeological site will realize, ancient people were well provided with dishes of all sorts. I would be very tempted, were it not for the great lapse of time, to make the claim that this was the very earliest form of pizza. Curiously, in that part of the world today, a flat thin bread garnished with ground meat and onions is still extremely popular.

The land that we now know as Italy was, in ancient times, a magnet for invaders attracted by the natural wealth and fertility of the countryside.

They brought with them their habits, their sensibilities, their food and their languages. Greek is still spoken in some southern Italian villages today. The happy result of these invasions is a great part of the intricate pattern of Italy's cuisine.

The areas of the peninsula that were colonized by the Greeks still delight in special breads spiced with oil, vinegar and herbs, and in stews made from fresh fish. These *frise* and *brodetti* of Apulia, and the pizza native to Naples and Campania, are echoed in France in the once Hellenic city of Marseilles with its *bouillabaise*, and in the *pan bagnat* and *fougasse* of that southern coast. Where the Etruscans flourished, they who relished gruel both soft and baked into cakes, today there is *polenta* and *schiacciata*, made by country women at their own firesides. The Arabs with their subtle traditions of bakery left delicate flaky pastries, now eaten in Naples as *sfogliatelle*. In Genoa, this art, seen in the lightest of savoury *torte*, was a secret which those seafarers brought back from journeys to Saracen lands.

With the ancient Greek civilisation we are approaching home ground; Naples, mythic burial place of the Siren Partenope, was part of *Magna Graecia* and was an important Hellenic city before the advent of the Romans. The Neapolitans have claimed pizza as their own invention to which they have a passionate attachment. To them it is much more than a simple food; it is a cult that brings a gleam to their eyes, a celebratory rite of the joy that they take in living. They feel a strong connection between themselves and their Greek and Roman forebears. Neapolitan scholars have woven ingenious and perhaps romantic webs to reinforce this connection between their joyous pizza and the ancient gods. My favourite of these theories concerns pizza, Demeter and the Eleusian Mysteries. The details of the rites of these Mysteries have been lost as only the initiates of the cult were permitted to know them, however in some way these ceremonies concerned flat loaves of bread.

The priestesses of the cult in Italy were chosen from among the Greek women of Naples and Veli. As part of their sacred duties they were allowed to accept ritual libations offered to the goddess by her devotees. These libations consisted of flour, water and a fragrant herb, probably mint or basil. The libation was mixed into a dough and then baked in flames, as was the babe Demophöon in the legend of Demeter's search for Core. A connection is then made between this sacred bread and *placenta*, a flat bread that was sold by the *placentari* in the streets of Naples and Pompeii. So pizza is said by some Italian scholars to be a direct descendant of Roman *placenta* and inspired by Demeter.

However fanciful this construction is, and I find it a delightful notion that modern pizza stems from the Cult of Isis–Ceres–Demeter, it still says something valuable about the Neapolitans and their regard for pizza. It is for them almost sacred in an ancient and pagan sense. And it is this sensibility and passion that has kept the presence of this simple flat bread, smeared with whatever savoury relish there was to hand, alive and vital. The dry pedantic following-through of semantic connections is hard tack compared to the thread of feeling that connects the revellers, the whores, the bakers, the humble and the rich of ancient Pompeii who ate the flat bread in the towns' many *trattorie*, with their descendants who still live with the acrid scent of Vesuvius in their nostrils and a sense of this link in their blood.

But as well as feeling, there are words that connect and one of the best sources is the work of the antiquarian Athenaeus. He was a Greek from Egyptian Naucratis who lived and wrote in Rome between the years 170 and 230 A.D. In his rambling *Deipnosphistae* (The Sophists at the Dinner Table), which is a massive and confected after-dinner conversation, he gives a fascinating list of diverse breads. The merits are discussed of fine oven-breads, brazier-bread, and the delightful allurement of Athenian smeared brazier-bread dipped in sweet wine to provoke a second appetite. *Laganon*, a light and thin wafer bread spoken of by Aristophanes, *artolaganon*, made with wine, pepper, milk, oil and lard, *plakitês*, a flat bread or cheese bread, Roman *'panis'*, and *artopticeus*, a bread that in some unspecified way was different in nature from those cooked in ovens and furnaces. The list continues for many pages. We also know that a *pistor* was a baker of loaves as was a *pistore* in 19th-century Italy, *panis focacius* was bread cooked on the hearth, the forerunner of our modern *focaccia*, *laganum* was a small cake of flour mixed with oil and *picentinus* was a bread made from spelt, and was much sought-after and made in Picentia, or so we are told by Pliny. Picentia is situated between Naples and Pozzuoli not far from Salerno, exactly in that area of Italy, Campania, that lays claim to be the cradle of pizza.

Today, many Italian cookery writers and historians agree that the pizza has descended in a simple form from the ancient Greeks and Romans. About a thousand years ago bread was called *lagano* in Naples, the word taken from the Greek *laganon* and the Latin *laganum* – a simple pizza is known by this name in Greece today. Shortly after the words *picea*, then *piza*, appear. To me, the ancient Greek and Roman *merenda* of bread eaten with a relish, Virgil's *moretum*, a simple circle of dough seasoned with oil, vinegar and sparked off with a little onion, was eaten in the same spirit as is a slice of pizza or a piece of hot *schiac-*

ciata munched hungrily on a cold morning in our century. If the trail is imprecise, the lively dish has survived.

There is a gap in the written sources on the subject of pizza until in the 18th and 19th centuries it emerges again from the world of the ordinary, the unremarkable, to appear in books and the journals of curious foreign travellers. Goethe visited Italy in the 1780s and has left us with a superb and sympathetic account of the country at that fascinating period in time when Naples was the golden city of Europe, rich, fat and fair. Naples was Goethe's 'incomparable city' with the 'Neapolitan crowd rushing by like a river', and this unsurpassed account shows the spirit of the vivid, ardent life in the city streets and the Neapolitan obsession with food.

There is no season when one is not surrounded on all sides by victuals. The Neapolitan not only enjoys his food, but insists that it be attractively displayed for sale. In Santa Lucia the fish are placed on a layer of green leaves, and each category – rock lobsters, oysters, clams and small mussels – has a clean, pretty basket to itself. But nothing is more carefully planned than the display of meat, which, since their appetite is stimulated by a periodic fast day, is particularly coveted by the common people.

In the butchers' stalls, quarters of beef, veal or mutton are never hung up without having the unfatty parts of the flanks and legs heavily gilded.

Several days in the year and especially the Christmas holidays are famous for their orgies of gluttony. At such times a general *cocagna* is celebrated, in which five hundred thousand people vow to outdo each other. The Toledo and other streets and squares are decorated most appetizingly; vegetables, raisins, melons and figs are piled high in their stalls; huge paternosters of gilded sausages, tied with red ribbons, and capons with little red flags stuck in their rumps are suspended in festoons across the streets overhead. I was assured that, not counting those which people had fattened in their own homes, thirty thousand of them had been sold. Crowds of donkeys laden with vegetables, capons and young lambs are driven to market, and never in my life have I seen so many eggs in one pile as I have seen here in several places. . .

. . . So far as flour-and-milk dishes are concerned, which our cooks prepare so excellently and in so many different ways, though people here lack our well-equipped kitchens and like to make short work of their cooking, they are catered for in two ways. The macaroni, the dough of which is made from a very fine flour, kneaded into various shapes and then boiled, can be bought everywhere and in all the shops for very little money. As a rule, it is simply cooked in water and seasoned with grated cheese. Then at almost every corner of the main streets, there are pastrycooks with their frying pans of sizzling oil, busy, especially on fast days, preparing pastry and fish on the spot for anyone who wants it. Their sales are fabulous, for thousands and thousands of people carry their lunch and supper home, wrapped in a little piece of paper.

Goethe *Italian Journey*

These little fried pastries and pieces of dough perhaps filled with seasonings are the forerunners of the *calzoncelli*, *pizzelle* and *panzarotti* for which we now have delicious recipes.

Goethe enjoyed his stay in Naples during the reign of the Bourbon King Ferdinando I and Queen Maria Carolina, daughter of the Empress Maria Teresa of Austria and sister of Marie Antoinette. Queen Carolina came from a country famous for its pastry cooks – they even invented the *croissant* as an insult to the Turks camped at their gates, showing that they intended to eat the Turkish crescent. Unlike her ill-fated sister, Maria Carolina had the common touch; she even liked eating pizza. Her first taste of it was brought to her by a courtier who carried it from the *Taverna del Cerriglio*, a famous Neapolitan inn and place of amorous assignation that was much frequented by townsfolk, courtiers and poets alike. Ferdinando then had a red-tiled pizza oven constructed at the Capo di Monte palace near the porcelain kilns so that the Queen and her companions might indulge their vulgar tastes and enjoy a picnic of pizza on warm summer evenings. Ferdinando had a more esoteric appetite – when upset or worried he would consume small pieces of paper inscribed with prayers and incantations.

Towards the 19th century and onwards pizza really comes into its own. From the observations of contemporary writers we know that itinerant pizza sellers roamed the crowded streets and teeming lanes of Naples. They displayed their wares on a simple board, cutting their pizza up into affordable slices with a knife in exactly the same way that the children of Goethe's Naples sold watermelon. Others carried the *pizze* in hexagonal metal boxes equipped with vented lids. These vendors would buy pizza *vullente*, boiling hot, from the ovens of a fixed pizza stand, and would go through the city crying their wares: *'C' 'o fungietiello e' alice! Na bona marenna!'*, 'With mushrooms or anchovies! What a good breakfast!' This particular cry was for summer mornings; the poor ate pizza for breakfast, lunch and dinner on weekdays and treated themselves to a helping of *maccheroni* on Sunday, again bought from a stall in a street.

The more prosperous *pizzaioli* had fixed stands in which were counters topped with cool marble. Here the dough was slapped into shape, seasoned with whatever the customers desired and cooked in the perpetually burning oven. Scaffolding shelves held various pots and jars full of seasonings like tomato (for by this time that most characteristic ingredient had established itself), cheese, basil, oregano, lard, pepper, oil and anchovies to substitute for expensive salt. Rough tables and chairs were provided for the customers as were, no doubt, copious supplies of wine from the vineyards on the slopes of Vesuvius. These stands must have been rather like the open air cafés selling watermelon that are still to be seen in the summer in many Italian cities.

The first real pizzeria in Naples was opened around the year 1830 near the Port Alba, and here workmen, students, artists and writers came to eat, sit and talk and some composed verses in honour of the golden discs of dough. Other *pizzerie* opened in competition and the owners would stand at their welcoming doors and sing out in melodious tones the merits of their wares: pizza, 'the yeast of life', 'the talisman of happiness', 'the soothing unguent for the weak of stomach'. In the old-fashioned *pizzerie* of Naples I have often heard pretty songs to pizza sung by itinerant street singers.

Alexander Dumas, the elder, who sojourned in Naples, wrote of pizza too and compared it to the round flat breads of St. Denis. He might also have recognized a similarity to a 19th-century Provençal recipe for *Pompe à l'Anchois* or *Fougasso à l'Anchoio*, a thrice-risen flat bread decorated with oil-moistened anchovies and baked in the *four de la Commune* at Christmas time. He took care to note that in Naples the *pizze* were seasoned with oil, lard, pork fat, cheese, tomato and tiny fish. He also mentioned a *pizza a otto*, which he assumed was baked eight days before it was eaten, a strange error seeing how easily a pizza becomes hard once stale. Actually *a otto* refers to a week's credit, as the pizza was paid for eight days after it was eaten; a great many things can happen to a person in eight days and probably did in the colourful Naples of the last century – your last pizza might even be a free one!

Much of our information about pizza in the 19th century comes from the writings of Emmanuele Rocca. Born in Spain in 1811, he was among the contributors to Francesco de Bourcard's famous *Usi e Costumi di Napoli e Contorni*, 1857 and 1866, one of the great number of books on popular ethnography that appeared in the mid 19th-century after the publication of E.W. Lane's *Manners and Customs of the Modern Egyptians*. At that period there was an insatiable curiosity about the habits and everyday lives of other peoples. Rocco tells us about the popular flavourings for pizza at that time.

> The most ordinary pizza, called *coll' aglio e l'oglio* (with garlic and oil), has for its seasoning oil, and on top they spread, besides the salt, oregano and finely chopped cloves of garlic. Others are covered with grated cheese and moistened with lard, and on top there are placed a few leaves of basil. To the first tiny fish are often added; to the second thin slices of mozzarella. Some use sliced prosciutto, tomato, clams, etc. Some fold the dough over on itself in a form which they call *calzone*.

Here at last we can truly recognize some famous *pizze*, though to be sure, tomato does not seem to hold undue importance.

The second Italian queen to elevate pizza was Margherita, wife of Umberto I of Savoia *'il re buono'* ('the good king'). Their wedding at Turin in 1868 when she was seventeen was a magnificent occasion and the couple immediately set out on a tour of Italy to see their future kingdom and to drum up some popular support for the monarchy. Margherita, in spite of her poor Italian, proved to have a genius for 'public relations'. To begin her career she secured a pardon for political prisoners. All through Italy the population fell in love with her; for the first time a traditionally cloistered royal princess kissed babies on a Bologna railway station, and at Genoa she drove through the city in a carriage wearing on her beautiful blonde hair a *pezzullo*, the local peasant headdress. In Venice, processing in a gondola, she wore the *zendado*, in Naples, Vesuvius was erupting but ceased on her arrival. The people decided that she brought good luck.

This queen, famous too for her fabulous pearls and splendid diamonds, and the whispered story that after catching Umberto *in flagrante delicto* with his mistress she never again graced his bed, also

IL PIZZAIUOLO.

LATTERIA
GIULIO MOGGI

loved the food of the people, the *pizza napoletana*. In June of 1889 Raffaele Esposito, owner of the celebrated pizzeria 'Pietro e . . . basta cosi', was invited to the royal palace where he made three sorts of pizza for the Queen to taste. Her favourite, the one dressed with tomato, mozzarella and basil, he named in her honour 'Margherita', and this pizza has travelled all over the world.

In our century the pizza has become ubiquitous, but its spread did not really begin until the 1950s. At this time many Neapolitans left their beloved city in search of work in northern Italy. They missed their *stemma comunale*, their emblem of the man in the street, so much that *pizzerie* started to open in the large cities to answer their need. Today there are several in most Italian towns – I counted twenty-two in Trento, a modest-sized town.

Pizzerie have largely taken the place of the old-fashioned *trattoria* and *taverna*, eating houses that were relaxed and informal. In these places ordinary people could eat simply and cheaply. The *latteria* provided a similar service but these white-tiled cafés which sold milk, coffee, but no wines or spirits, and where in Milan in the 1950s you could eat a substantial two-course meal for two hundred lire, have now totally disappeared at any tariff. The *latterie* were found in ordinary city streets and were frequented by tradesmen, shop workers and students, in short, the not very well-off.

Neapolitans who left their native soil in search of new lives in North and South America took the pizza with them.

> If you patronized a local Italian eatery, then chances were that one of your favourite dishes was what was then called 'ah-beetz', that flat, round pie of tomatoes and 'mootz-a-*rell*' cheese, which has since become the national fast food favourite we now know as pizza. In those days the signs and menus spelled it 'apizza' and it could be bought only as a full pie served at a table, in the back, at the end of the bar.
>
> Elliot Willensky
> *When Brooklyn Was The World 1920-1957*

Today in New York pizza has become an acceptable form of fast food, as cheap and nourishing as it has always been. Very soon a chain of pizza houses will open in the U.S.S.R. In Britain since the 1970s pizza houses, good, dreadful and indifferent, have proliferated and show no signs of losing their popularity. I have an Italian friend who says that the thick crust of some British *pizze* is just like that of the old-fashioned Neapolitan pizza. But, as it always has, pizza still graces the tables of the rich and sophisticated. The fashionable restaurants in the great cities of the United States offer what American food writers call 'designer' pizza and *calzoni*, made carefully out of the most subtle cheeses married to other rare and delicate flavours.

> Pizza? Oh Lord, yes, pizza is definitely on the menu. In fact, I suspect that pizza will always be on the menu. But of more significance than the goat cheese, Scotch smoked salmon and exotic mushrooms that are replacing tomato sauce on stylish little rounds of dough, is what the upscaling of pizza represents. It is one of the most obvious examples of a fundamental change occurring in American restaurants: a blurring of distinctions between fast-food restaurants and the so-called white tablecloth restaurants. When pizza goes on the menu of stylish restaurants and when elegant restaurants offer wild mushroom strudel to go – well, we're talking about a new ball game . . . I don't know of anything that is more quintessentially eighties than getting on in the world – unless, of course, its another slice of designer pizza.
>
> Stanley Dry
> Restaurant Column
> *Food and Wine* (New York, July 1985)

The long progress of pizza is one of the world's great success stories.

DOUGH
AND
BAKING

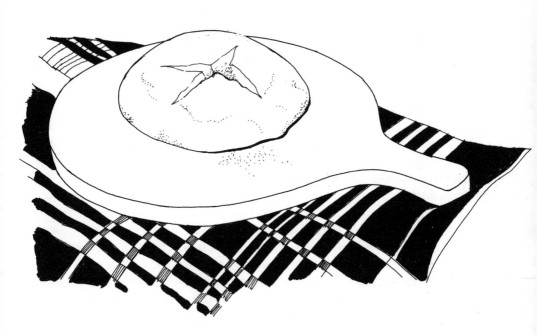

THE PIZZA DOUGH

DOUGH INGREDIENTS

Dough is the heart of the pizza. The crust must be light but chewy and have the nutty flavour of well-proved dough made from good flour.

Classic Italian pizza dough contains nothing but flour, yeast, salt and water. It is important to know which type of flour is the most suitable for making Italian bread and pizza dough and why.

Flour

In Italy nearly all bread flour is made from soft wheats called *grano tenero*, and flour is divided into five grades according to how much of the husk and whole grain has been bolted away.

All these categories were laid down in a law passed in Italy in 1967, and this law also specified the nature of a loaf of common bread thus: 'The product obtained from the cooking of risen dough, prepared with wheat flour, water and yeast, with or without the addition of common salt.' Bread, pure and simple.

The most refined flour, which comes under the category OO, is used in the making of special table breads, the French type of bread, cakes and pastries. Professional pizza makers use it because they like to make a fine supple dough which bakes well in the high temperatures of their ovens. It is easily available in all food stores and housewives use it for pasta and cake making, but not for pizza. Next comes the O grade, used commercially for *pane comune*, and commonly used by housewives for making home-made bread, *schiacciata* and pizza. It is a bulkier flour, giving a better result in the more modest temperatures of the domestic oven. Grade 1 flour is used for *pugliese*, *toscano* and *casereccio* loaves, and is coarser, darker and contains more of the whole wheat grain. I have never seen Grade 1 flour for sale to the general public. Grade 2, which is darker still, is very rare. *Integrale* or wholewheat flour has become much more popular in modern Italy for health reasons but wholewheat bread will not, I think, ever replace the white rough, crusty saltless loaves that are the daily bread in Tuscany.

In England, unbleached strong white flour, which is now widely available, makes the best pizza dough. Strong white flour contains a mixture of soft, usually home-grown wheat, which has a good flavour, and hard imported wheats with a high gluten, that is protein, content. The gluten allows the flour to absorb water, which in turn makes the dough expand, and so, with the help of the leavening qualities of yeast, you produce a bigger loaf with a firm structure. When strong white flour is unbleached and fresh, that is, untouched by time or chlorine, it has a lovely creamy hue, a characteristic flavour and its own natural supply of Vitamin B.

Ordinary refined bleached household flour, made solely from soft wheats with a low gluten content and with nearly all traces of bran and whole wheat grain sifted away, is only suitable for making cakes and pastries which do not need a bouncy dough or great volume for easy success.

Wholewheat flour, although healthy, flavourful and fashionable, is not typical or indeed suitable in real Italian pizza dough. Its distinctive flavour would compete too much with the strongly flavoured modern pizza seasonings to the disservice of both dough and topping.

Of the many sorts of flours available to the home cook in America, the unbleached all-purpose flour which has a mixture of soft and hard wheats is probably the most suitable for the recipes in this book.

Cooks in Britain and the United States are fortunate in being able to obtain high gluten strong flours which make bread and pizza making simple. Italian cooks need all their skill to manage their less powerful and less responsive flours. Very recently one or two large pasta manufacturers have started to market special mixtures of high and low gluten flours to make the housewives' task easier but even these flours do not match what is available in Britain and America.

Yeast

When I was a child and my Welsh grandmother baked our bread each week, she bought her yeast from the baker, Mr. Lewis. I enjoyed carrying it home and opening the paper package to sniff at the heady smell of the putty-coloured fist-sized lump, and I was even encouraged to eat a little raw as Grandma believed, quite correctly, that it was good for me.

Now, in this regulated world, yeast comes in neat silver paper-covered cubes. In Italy, where yeast is called *lievito di birra*, the cubes weigh 25 grams and have the date of usage stamped on the side. They are easily obtained from any small grocery store. In America and also in Britain similar raw compressed yeast, the putty-coloured and textured substance that one must cream, is available fairly readily. What is much more easily found in the United States and Britain are packages of granular dried active baking yeast. Yeast in this granular form is easy to store, lasts for a great deal of time and gives excellent results if you follow one basic rule: use half or less than half the quantity of dried yeast than you would need of fresh yeast. As is printed on the side of my can of proprietary dried yeast, 1 oz/28 g of dried active baking yeast is equal to 2 oz/56 g of fresh yeast.

Half a teaspoon of yeast granules will be quite sufficient to aerate the 10½ oz, 300 g or three cups of flour specified in a great many of the recipes in this book.

Recently a new yeast product has appeared on the British market, in the form of a powder which is simply sprinkled into the flour and so does not need to be dissolved before it is used. It does not work with Italian low gluten flours, as it is much too powerful. However, it works well with strong flour, but again, half a teaspoon is quite sufficient for most of the recipes in this book.

If you are not certain of the age or potency of the yeast that you are using dissolve it in the appropriate amount of warm water, add a small pinch of sugar and wait for five or ten minutes until the mixture fizzes and foams and gives off a barmy scent. If the yeast does not come to life throw it away.

Salt

Salt is the magic ingredient that sparks off the nutty taste of the flour in bread. Traditional Tuscan bread is perhaps the only type that does without salt and this is possibly because salt would attract moisture and mould to the loaves which were baked once a week and sometimes less often; mould would mean wastage, anathema to the thrifty Tuscan heart. Salt was also subject to government tax and expensive. An underlying reason for omitting salt may also be because it can inhibit the action of the yeast. This would make the already hard job of raising the dough in a cold northern Italian house then carrying it outside to the oven in perhaps inclement weather even more difficult. Savour was, and is, easily added to the bread by eating it with salty *prosciutto* and *salame*, sprinkling on *extra vergine* olive oil and a spray of coarse salt, and by dipping it into a tasty soup. In 19th-century Naples pizza was very often given its savour by anchovies preserved in salt.

Italian salt is marine salt and comes in two sorts, *fino* and *grosso*. The fine variety is coarser than British table salt but it nevertheless appears on Italian tables and in their kitchens, and has an excellent flavour. The coarse salt which comes in hard pieces the size of discreet diamonds is used more for curing hams and salting vegetable and pasta water. It is difficult to dissolve and is not used on pizza. Outside Italy a coarse but not rock-like plain sea salt is the best to use in these recipes. In Britain, crushed Maldon salt is perfect.

Liquids

The only liquid in classic Italian pizza dough is water. Quality of water is important: the softer the water the better the result. Hard water contains minerals which add unnecessary flavours; town water that has been heavily treated with chlorine also imparts its ugly flavour to food. Italians are extremely particular about their drinking water and each year countless litres of various types of *acqua minerale* are consumed. They will also drive many kilometres to famous mountain springs armed with *tanakas* to collect exceptionally good water, usually rich in some trace element that is recommended for various health conditions. Italian bakers rightly believe that sweet water is essential to the baking of good bread. Tuscans believe that their bread is superior to Umbrian bread because Tuscan water is sweeter.

Classic pizza dough responds best to the high heat of a professional pizza oven. Some *pizzaioli*, however, use milk instead of water to produce a smoother dough; some use olive oil to improve the texture and colour. Pizza dough made in Italian homes often includes olive oil, which makes the dough easier to knead and to bake better in a domestic oven.

Additions and Embellishments

The austere description of the nature of a loaf of common bread given in the Italian law of 1967 of course refers to a basic loaf. The law also permits what are called special breads. And these allow ample room for the flowering of the traditions and imagination of Italian bakers. There are myriads of festive breads that contain such things as spices, pepper, cheeses, scraps of pork left after the rendering down of fat for lard, raisins, fresh grapes, olives, oregano, aniseed, malt, butter, olive oil, lard, onion, tomato and rosemary. In short, any suitable seasoning that would raise a daily staple into a special treat. Italian women have always used whatever flavourings they had to enliven their hearthbreads.

RISING

Many people are apprehensive of yeast cookery, are put off by the mysterious process of leavening and assume that bread dough is difficult to handle. People leading busy lives also think the process laborious and time-consuming, but dough is patient; it will happily sit in its warm bowl and wait for you.

Yeast needs a warm moist atmosphere to develop and transform the dough into a puffy white pillow. The warmer the environment is, the faster the rising will be. Dough left at a room temperature of about

65°F/22°C will rise nicely overnight and give a good flavoured bread. A temperature of 85° to 90°F/30° to 32°C, which is the upper limit at which dough will flourish, can produce complete rising in less than thirty minutes, but with a loss of flavour.

In an Italian farmhouse the *massaia*, the matriarch, would make the week's bread supply in her *madia*, an oblong, wooden lidded trough on tall legs in which the dough was mixed and kneaded then left overnight to rise. Temperatures in the thick stone-walled country houses are never high whether summer or winter, so the bread rose slowly, but the slow rising produced a better flavour. The dough was protected from draughts, which would delay or stop the rising, by the enclosing walls of the bread chest. Just as country people look at the sun to tell them the time, it would not have occurred to them to measure the room temperature with a thermometer; bread just rose if certain rules, passed down from mother to daughter, were followed.

Modern centrally-heated houses of course make the whole process much easier. It is possible to hasten or hold back a dough to suit your own timetable and if you are not ready to bake, the dough will suspend its activity in the refrigerator. An oven with a pilot light will bring it along splendidly. With some annoyance I have to admit that in my own draughty stone farmhouse I have achieved better results using a light polythene mixing bowl than with pottery bowls and crocks, as the plastic seems more conducive to warmth. Today Italian women in the cities have all the advantages of central heating, but for their country grandmothers and great grandmothers baking presented much hard work and not a few problems.

Putting your dough into a large plastic mixing bowl (it must be large enough to take the expanding volume), covering it with a light plastic bag and leaving it in a draught-free corner of a warm kitchen should produce a well-risen dough in an hour or so. Do not be concerned so much with the time, it is the volume that you must measure. In very cold weather warm your flour and the bowl before starting to make the dough.

BAKING

The type of oven is the crucial factor in producing perfect *pizza alla Napoletana*. Professional *pizzaioli* bake in dome-shaped brick ovens with stone or brick floors. The *pizze* are laid straight on to these hot floors, which gives the baked dough its characteristic texture, a pleasant bread-like crust. The heat achieved in the brick ovens is very high, somewhere between 400° and 500°C. A pizza cooks in about four minutes and this brief contact with the dry, extremely hot brick floor and the dry heat of the oven produces a light chewy crust that has not had time to harden. The fragrant wood used to fire the ovens also adds an inimitable flavour to the *pizze*.

However, even with the limitations in the range of heat that it is possible to achieve in a normal domestic oven, we can still make successful and delicious *pizze*. A 425°F/220°C/7 temperature with the oven brought to its full heat before the pizza is put in on the middle shelf is probably most suitable. Anything higher will still not be hot enough to cook the pizza quickly but thoroughly, and will just serve to dry out the seasoning. At 425°F/220°C/7 a happy medium is reached; the crust should still be tender and the seasoning juicy. Each oven, of course, has its own quirks and tricks; the temperature that I have suggested is a guide and should be altered to suit the individual case. Italian cookery books seldom specify exact temperatures beyond suggesting a hot or medium oven, occasionally a *roventissimo*, that is, a roaring scorching heat. This is because the oven with an accurate temperature control is quite a recent development in the Italian kitchen. For pizza, many Italian manuals simply suggest a hot oven.

Round pizza can be cooked perfectly well on a flat well-proved pizza tin; the darker the tin is, the better the underside of the crust will bake. It will help too if the tin is placed on a baking sheet that has been allowed to heat up with the oven. A shallow oblong tray of pizza can also be successfully and conveniently baked in the same way and this will serve to feed several people at once. The round or square trays are easy to manoeuvre in and out of the hot oven.

However, there is another way of baking that will give a more authentic texture to the pizza and that is by using a baking stone or laying some flat unglazed floor tiles on the oven rack. Putting unformed loaves of bread on these tiles, too, will give a lovely crust to the bottom of the loaf.

In Britain around the turn of the century some of the newly arrived gas and electric ovens were equipped with tile bottoms so that cottage loaves could still be baked with the customary pleasant crust that was achieved in the old brick bread ovens. At that time of course people still baked their own bread to a great extent, and it was important that these new ovens should perform the old tasks well. Perhaps with today's renewed interest in home baking and real bread some enterprising manufacturer might consider designing something similar. Until then unglazed floor tiles are easily available. In Italy baking stones are still to be found (as they are, I believe, in the United States), but are used on the open fire. For more details about them please refer to the section on *schiacciata* and hearthbreads (See pages 118 to 134).

If you choose to use tiles or a baking stone you must put them into the oven and heat them for half an hour before you put the pizza in to bake. Therefore you must roll out your circle of dough and lay it on a floured board or a floured sheet of cardboard to prove, dress it with your choice of ingredients and then slip the pizza from the board or card on to the hot tiles or bakestone. This is quite an easy feat to accomplish with very little practise. Professional *pizzaioli* and bakers put their wares into the oven with the aid of a long-handled flat wooden shovel called a *pala* in Italy and a peel in Britain. They take out the pizza with a smaller round metal shovel also equipped with a long handle.

I have found a drawback, however, to using tiles when baking an open pizza with a generous and liquid seasoning. The topping can easily escape on to the tiles and afterwards the oil is difficult to remove, with the result that the next time you bake there can be a dreadful smell. In fact I tend to use tiles more for baking breads, *schiacciate* and *calzone*.

A criticism often levelled at Italian pizza crust is that it becomes tough when cold. Pizza crust is not meant to become cold, it is intended to be eaten scorchingly hot straight from the oven when it is at its absolute best. No respectable Neapolitan would keep left-over pizza and attempt to reheat it; the style, the enjoyment, the whole point of the dish would be lost. Like a soufflé, pizza has a life; it is eaten at its high point or it dies. If a lighter, more delicate dish is indicated then housewives will made a savoury *torta*, a tart, out of *pasta frolla*, a fleur pastry made from flour, butter, egg yolk, lemon juice and iced water.

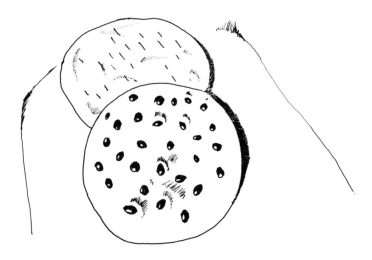

PASTA PER PIZZA
PIZZA DOUGH

To make pizza dough you will need 10½ oz/3 cups/300 g of unbleached **flour**
strong white flour or American all-purpose flour; 1 heaped teaspoon of **yeast**
salt; ½ teaspoon of active dried yeast granules plus ½ teaspoon of sugar, **olive**
oil
or ½ oz/15 g of compressed fresh yeast; 6 fl oz/¾ cup/175 ml of hand-hot **sugar**
water; a generous tablespoon of fruity olive oil. **salt**
water

The amount of dough yielded from this recipe will be sufficient to make two medium-size 11 to 12 inch round *pizze*, 1 oblong tray of pizza 10 by 14 inches or twelve small 4 inch *pizzette* or *pizzelle*.

Mix the unsifted flour and the salt in a large warm bowl. Pour into a glass a little of the hand-hot water; it should be neither tepid nor hot to the touch. (It is worth remembering that if the glass is very cold it will immediately reduce the temperature of the water.) With a fork, whisk the yeast granules plus the sugar into the water until they are dissolved. If you are using compressed yeast crumble it with your fingers and mix it with a spoon into the water until it too has dissolved. Leave the yeast mixture for about ten minutes in a warm place until it is fizzy and creamy and gives off a barmy smell.

Next, make a well in the heap of flour and pour in the yeast mixture and an overflowing tablespoon of olive oil. Start to bring the dough together by pushing the flour down into the liquid. Mix it with a fork, adding the rest of the water little by little until you are left with a rough ball of dough. The quantity of water needed depends entirely on the absorbancy of the particular flour – the amount specified in the recipe is a guide. You will feel how much water you need. If the dough is sticky add a sprinkling of flour; if there are drifts of dry flour in the bowl add extra water, a little at a time. When the dough has come together in a ball leaving the sides of the bowl clean, take it out and put it on a flat, lightly floured work surface.

Now you can begin to knead the dough until it has a lithe and silky texture. Do this by pushing at the dough with the heels of your hands, turning it over and around rhythmically, pressing the dough like a cat kneading a cushion. Gradually the texture will change under your hands and the dough will become soft and elastic; this will take about eight to ten minutes.

Next, put the ball of dough into a large clean bowl that you have lightly sprinkled with flour, and make a cross cut on the top of the ball of dough with a sharp knife. This will open the surface and aid the dough to rise. (Country women in Italy used to do this to keep away the evil spirits and at one time the lack of a cross on their dough meant that they were taken for witches.) Sprinkle a little more flour on top of the dough, cover the bowl closely with a plastic bag and leave it in a warm draught-free place to rise until it is doubled in volume. This will take from one to three hours depending on the room temperature.

When you are ready to assemble your pizza you must 'knock back' the puffy ball of dough. Do this by gently punching the air out of it with your fist, then gather the dough together, lay it on the floured work surface and knead it for a few minutes. If you want to make two round *pizze*, break the ball of dough in half, make a ball of each half and flatten it into a disc with your hands, then either roll it out with a rolling pin or press it with your fingers into the required shape. It should be about an eighth of an inch thick, thickening a little towards the edges. If you want to make *pizzette*, little individual *pizze*, divide the dough into twelve balls and flatten them out in the same way.

The process for lining an oblong tin is a little different. Here you must roll out the dough into roughly the required shape, lay it in the lightly oiled tin and press the dough out with your fingertips and knuckles until it fills the entire surface right into the corners and slightly up the edges to make a neat retaining wall. Let the dough rest and rise a little for a second time while the oven heats.

The *pizze* or *pizzette* can be left on lightly oiled flat tins, or floured boards (if you choose to bake on tiles) for a second rising when the dough will relax and come to life again after all the handling it has gone through. While the dough rests, your oven should be heating to its full temperature and when that is achieved you may dress the *pizze* according to the recipes given in further chapters.

Baking with instant powdered yeast
If you wish to use instant powdered yeast, simply mix half a teaspoon of it into the dry flour and salt, then proceed to add the olive oil and water and continue to follow the recipe as given above.

Dressing the pizza
The crust and the seasoning on a pizza should fuse together in the heat of the oven making a juicy whole, so the seasoning should be nicely balanced in quantity; neither meagre nor overwhelming. The texture

and flavour of the diverse ingredients must complement and enhance each other. A pizza is a complete dish in itself so the eater must not become bored by too bland a seasoning or surfeited by a too rich or overspiced array. Above all a pizza is not a convenient dumping ground for all manner of odds and ends lurking at the back of the refrigerator. Excellent fresh ingredients chosen and used with discretion make a good pizza.

ON USING THE RECIPES

QUANTITIES

In Italy when eating at a pizzeria Italians expect to have a large round pizza about 11 to 12 inches in size all to themselves as a one-course meal. When baking pizza at home for the family they will generally make an oblong tray of pizza which can be cut into portions to feed several people at once. This is because of the limitations in size of the normal domestic oven; you cannot get more than one 12 inch round pizza on to the required oven shelf.

When I serve pizza for two or three people I like to bake two round *pizze*, each with different toppings; while we divide and eat the first, the second one is baking. For larger groups an oblong tray of pizza is preferable, or perhaps small *pizzette*.

Courtyard of an Umbrian Pizzeria

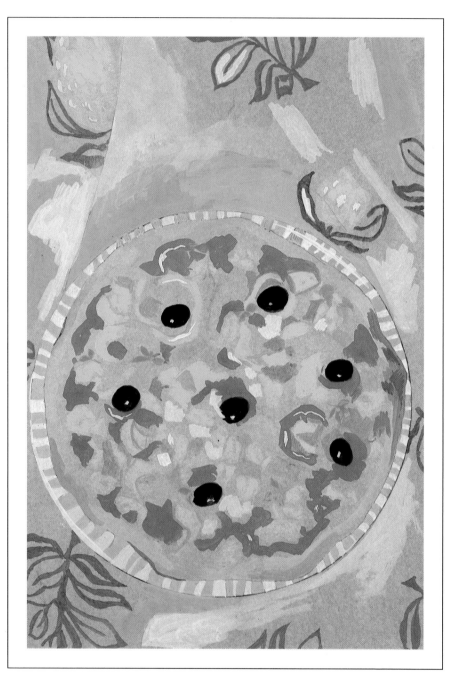

Pizza with golden peperoni and fresh marjoram

The quantities of dough that I have suggested in the master recipe on page 29 is sufficient for two medium-size 11 to 12 inch *pizze*, one tray 10 by 14 inches, or twelve small 4 inch *pizzette*. The quantities in the pizza topping recipes, except where otherwise stated, will cover one 11 to 12 inch pizza. To cover an oblong tray you will need double the quantities of the main ingredients, but a little less than double the amount of strong seasonings such as anchovies, olives and herbs.

I do not recommend making very large batches of dough as they are much harder to handle and you will require a very large bread crock to contain the expanded mass. It is worthwhile to remember that when doubling the quantity of flour and liquid in a recipe it is not necessary to double the amount of yeast. The less you use, the better the texture of the crust will be. Too much yeast gives dry bread.

MEASUREMENTS

All quantities in the recipes are given in imperial pounds and ounces, American cups and metric kilos and grams. Whichever type of measurement is chosen (i.e. imperial or cups), it is important to keep to that measurement throughout the recipe. Teaspoons and tablespoons are American-sized, which are roughly equivalent to 5 ml and 15 ml metric spoons respectively.

EQUIPMENT

All that is absolutely necessary to make pizza is a bowl large enough to take an expanding mass of dough, a flat round pizza tin or an oblong baking tray and an efficient oven. I make my pizza dough by hand as it gives me pleasure to do so. However, use a food mixer with a dough hook if it pleases you; follow the manufacturer's instructions for mixing dough.

FREEZING

I do not possess a freezer as I do not care for frozen food. To my taste its texture and flavour is irredeemably impaired, besides I prefer to wait for the special enjoyment of eating fresh peas in June instead of indulging in the dubious pleasures of frozen peas in December. It is possible to successfully freeze raw dough after the first rising for about one to two weeks. As it takes several hours to thaw, one may as well start from scratch and, like the Italians, produce fresh dough when it is needed.

FATS AND OILS, OLIVES, CAPERS, HERBS, SPICES

These ingredients, used in smaller quantities than the main items on a pizza, serve to moisten, give zest and add extra flavour.

FATS AND OILS

The only fat traditionally used on pizza is lard. A nut of lard is sometimes used to moisten the dough before the tomato and other seasonings are added. For an example, notice the recipe for *Pizza alla Napoletana* on page 44. Occasionally lard is used in some hearthbreads and *piadine*. However, you can successfully substitute olive oil or butter for lard.

Olive oil is indispensable, there is no substitute for it in the making of a genuine flavourful Italian pizza. No other oil can compare with it for flavour and versatility. Nor is there any substitute for it in the diverse sauces and preserves for which recipes appear at different points in this book. The type and provenance of the oil is important. Italians prefer *olio extra vergine d'oliva* for salads and dishes in which the oil is prominent; this oil, according to a law passed in Italy in 1960, must not contain more than one percent oleic acid. It is a pure oil that has not been treated with chemicals, is easily digested and has a fine flavour. Italians also use *olio di oliva*, which has a higher acid content, in other types of dishes. For a robust recipe where a strongly flavoured oil is indicated, a Tuscan or Umbrian *extra vergine* oil is suitable. For delicately flavoured dishes such as the *Torta Pasqualina* on page 148, an oil from Liguria, which, owing perhaps to the nature of the soil, is a lighter, more delicate oil akin to French olive oils, would be the one to choose. For special salads and dishes where oil plays a very important part, such as the dressing for a plate of *bresaola* and rocket (arugula), an *olio extra vergine di prima spremitura*, the oil obtained from the first cold pressing of the olives, is often used. This more expensive type of oil usually comes from famous Chianti vintners who also have olive groves.

I have heard and read admiring comments on oil that has a peppery throat-burning effect. According to my Tuscan neighbours who harvest their own olives for oil, and friends who buy their oil in bulk from farmers, this peppery aftertaste is a defect, a disaster that can occasionally befall. Olive oil should be of an ineffable sweetness.

When buying oil in Britain and the United States, it is usual to find *extra vergine* oil and simple olive oil side by side on shop shelves. It is really worth the difference in price to buy the *extra vergine*, which will have a deeper, richer olive flavour. Choose the *extra vergine* that is sold in a clear glass bottle, not in a can, so you can see its colour. Italian oil tends to be better when it has a deep tone, although farmers have been known to steep olive leaves in the oil to enliven the colour. Avoid pale yellowish Italian olive oil as it is usually too refined and flavourless. French oils, on the other hand, may be pale but still have a lively flavour. Good olive oil is a magic ingredient that can transform a simple soup or a few steamed vegetables into an absolute delight, and it is worth every penny spent on it.

OLIVES

Most olives, whether they are gathered green and unripe or black and fully ripened, are bitter. To remove the *oleuropeina*, the bitter element, they have to be either treated with chemicals and then kept in brine, or simply kept in brine for a long period of time before they become mild, a process called in Italy *dolcificazione*, sweetening.

Both green and black olives are used on pizza. They are generally plain olives conserved in brine and are not enriched with herbs and extra flavourings. *Olive toste*, oven-dried olives, are also not used on pizza as they would become too hard in the baking. When added to an already heavily flavoured pizza, the clear taste of a juicy olive is what is needed and is what Italians use. However, for a simple antipasto of a few olives with a little cheese and a glass of wine it is pleasant to have olives that have been marinated in oil flavoured with a little thyme. My favourite Umbrian way of serving olives is to mix together plump black ones with orange peel cut into tiny dice, a little finely chopped garlic and a bay leaf crumbled into fragments. The mixture should be left to soak in olive oil for twenty-four hours for the flavours to develop. The glistening black olives look handsome mixed with the bright orange of the peel, the dull green of the bay and the white garlic.

Recipes in which olives play an important part like *Schiacciata con Cipolle ed Ulive* can be found on page 129 and in *Focaccia con Le Olive Verde* on page 132.

Polpa d'Oliva *Crushed Olive Pulp*
This is a soft paste made from the crushed flesh of black or porphyry-coloured mild olives. When mixed with mozzarella it makes an interesting and savoury addition to a pizza, for an example notice *Pizza con La Mozzarella e Polpa d'Oliva* on page 60.

In Italy the paste, sold in small glass jars, can be obtained from many food stores, however it is possible to make your own by pitting mild black olives conserved in brine, chopping the pulp, then blending it in a blender with a little olive oil and perhaps some anchovy, oregano or a few flakes of hot chilli pepper. As well as using this mixture on a pizza it also makes an excellent pasta sauce when spiked with garlic and is good on *crostini*, small rounds of toasted or plain bread covered with the paste and served as an antipasto. If you mix two to three tablespoons of plain *polpa d'oliva* into the dough for a *schiacciata* (see the master recipe on page 122), adding the pulp at the second kneading before forming the dough into the flat bread, it will make an interesting *Genovese focaccia*.

CAPERS *Capparis Rupestris or Spinosa*
Capers are the small unopened buds of a pretty flowering plant which grows in self-seeded clusters clinging to the crevices of ancient stone walls all over the Mediterranean region. The flowers are a delicate

green-tinted white and have long dangling purple stamens. I have heard that in Spain there is one variety that is extremely poisonous. In Italy the buds are usually preserved in wine vinegar, in which case they must be immersed in it for ten days, then removed and packed into small jars and covered with fresh salted wine vinegar. They can also be preserved in salt but for this they have to be picked with a little of the stem still attached, then laid in the hot sun for an hour or so to dry a little. After this they are put into jars with alternating layers of salt, the jars to be filled to the top with the last layer a salt one.

When salted capers are used they should be well washed and care must be taken in the seasoning of the dish they are to adorn. Capers go into the splendid *salsa verde*, the green sauce that accompanies one of the great Italian dishes, the *bollito misto*, served from a *carrello* equipped with massive silver domed lids which hide the various boiled meats, capon or hen, beef, tongue, *cotechino*, sometimes mortadella and *zampone*. The sauce is made from copious amounts of chopped parsley, capers, garlic and olive oil and it is the capers that give the sauce its distinctive and refreshing quality.

Capers also appear on *pizze* and add a fresh acid note to enliven the general flavour. Recipes on pages 47 and 97.

HERBS

Various herbs are used to perfume pizza and the general rule to follow is to use fresh herbs whenever possible.

Oregano or wild marjoram, Lat. *origanum vulgare,* It. *origano*, is used on many Neapolitan *pizze*. It is essential on *pizza alla Napoletana* and in various *calzoni* and *paste fritti*. However, the quality of the oregano is vital. Oregano picked wild or from your garden and then used fresh or carefully dried on the stalk, at home, is a wonderful herb. But, it must only be kept until its scent begins to dissipate. Dried crumbled oregano bought in a cardboard box at a supermarket generally has a rancid smell and makes a pizza taste like cheap scented soap. Better to do without and add a little thyme.

Thyme, Lat. *thymus vulgaris,* It. *timo*, picked from the garden, can be used fresh or dried as it does not have a musty smell like that of dried sage which ruins so many stuffings intended to enhance roast chicken.

Parsley, Lat. *petroselinum sativum,* It. *prezzemelo*, must be used fresh whether it is the flat-leaved Mediterranean sort or the curly variety. When buying parsley try and obtain young tender sprigs; a great deal of it that appears in greengrocers is too tough and wiry. Dried parsley is useless unless you care for green dust on your food.

Sweet marjoram, Lat. *origanum majorana,* It. *maggiorana*, should be used fresh, the small green leaves added after the pizza is baked. It is used to contrast with dried oregano, for an example see the recipe on page 75 and page 148, where the herb is used to advantage in *Torta Pasqualina.*

Basil, Lat. *ocymum basilicum,* It. *basilico*, is used fresh when the scent of the soft luxurious green leaves is at its strongest. It can be dried for use in the winter but much of the flavour is dissipated. If you want to use dried basil it is best to dry it yourself, as commercial dried basil is another snare, generally dusty and tasteless. To dry basil pick the largest and fleshiest leaves from the plants, as these will hold their scent longer, then lay them singly on sheets of brown paper. Let them lie in a warm room and when they are desiccated but still green put them in a clean glass jar and close it with a fairly loose-fitting cork stopper. You can also store them in an ordinary paper bag hung in a dry and airy place. Basil grows well in pots on a sunny window ledge. When on a visit to Italy buy new basil seed to take home and sow; it is a beautiful plant that will reward you with wafts of its scent when you water it.

Sage, Lat. *salvia officinalis,* It. *salvia*. Use sage only when it is fresh and then choose the tender pale green leaves from the new growth; in this way it has a soft pleasant flavour. It is excellent when warmed in melted butter and used to season *ravioli* filled with ricotta and spinach. In Tuscany there is an old dish called *salvietta* designed to celebrate the new sage. It is a simple béchamel studded with tiny sage leaves and baked in a buttered dish in the oven. New sage leaves are also delicious when used on a *schiacciata* like that on page 123.

Mint. Many varieties of mint are used in Italian cooking, like *menta comune*, Lat. *mentha viridis*, Eng. spearmint, commonly called *erba menta* or *menta romana*; *menta puleggio*, Lat. *mentha pulegium*, Eng. penny royal, often called *mentuccia*, with tiny spade-shaped leaves and pale purple flowers, and *mentastro*, Lat. *mentha aquatica*, Eng. water mint, also known as *menta rossa* from its red stems. In Rome common spearmint, *menta comune*, goes into a delicious dish baked in an earthenware pot which consists of layers of sliced courgettes alternated with layers of mint bathed in olive oil. Small-leaved wild penny royal mint, *mentuccia*, is used to flavour wild mushrooms, but I believe that the *nepitella* that the Tuscans pick when they go hunting for *porcini* as the natural flavouring for the *funghi* is closer to a wild savory. Mint provides a green note in the recipe for preserved aubergines (eggplants) given on page 82. Mint should be used fresh.

Borage, Lat. *borago officinalis,* It. *borragine*, is used in *torta d'erbe*, the pie made from ricotta and green leaf vegetables for which a recipe is given in a later chapter of this book (see page 152). The tender leaves of this wild plant are collected to make salads and *frittate;* the tougher ones are cooked like spinach, and the pretty little purple flowers decorate salads and are also candied.

Sorrel, Lat. *rumex acetosa,* It. *acetosa*, is collected wild by country people and used to flavour egg dishes and salads. It, too, goes into many *torte d'erbe*.

We in northern Europe and the United States have a very sparing almost puritanical attitude towards fresh herbs. It is interesting to note that the proportions of the various vegetables and herbs that are sold in the markets of the Middle East are quite different from the amounts offered in Western greengroceries and markets. Whilst we consider it normal to have large sacks of vegetables and maybe a punnet filled with a few dispirited sprigs of sage and small bundles of curly parsley which are meanly weighed by the ounce, in Middle Eastern lands the bundles of startlingly green parsley are immense because such herbs form a very important part of their cooking. Indeed, in Turkey, conventional salad greens are not in great evidence; instead you are served with great bowls of fresh mint leaves, fresh parsley, wild thyme and dandelion leaves, all of which are eaten in the quantities that one would normally consume the insipid lettuce. What we reserve as a sparingly used flavouring they eat in generous amounts accompanied by the acid tang of real yoghurt and flat unleavened breads. In Italy, one often sees in markets whole stalls devoted to herbs, either sold in the form of sturdy plants set in terracotta pots, or young seedlings lovingly wrapped in damp newspaper. Italians take herbs seriously.

SPICES
Black pepper, Lat. *piper nigrum,* It. *pepe nere*, appears in nearly all the recipes in this book. It should be freshly ground in a small pepper mill, as ready-ground pepper loses its aroma very quickly. When buying black peppercorns examine them carefully, very often corns of diverse qualities are mixed together. Choose the pot or jar that has a predominance of fat black berries, as small brown ones are of inferior quality.

In one or two recipes white pepper is recommended. This is solely to enhance the appearance of the dish, as a pale sauce is not improved by small black specks.

Chilli peppers, Lat. *capsicum frutescens,* It. *peperoncino.* These are small dried red peppers and are exceedingly hot. They are sometimes sold in Italian markets still attached to their withered plants and one can hang the branch or garland from the beams of the kitchen ceiling and pick off a pepper when it is needed. They are also sold in jars either whole or crushed. In Italy, particularly in the south, they are used a great deal in pasta sauces like *penne arrabiata* and *spaghetti alla putanesca* and they are also used to flavour long thin Neapolitan *salami*, often made from a variety of meats including horse meat. In Tuscany *peperoncino* is called *zenzero*, the result of an ancient confusion of terms. On a pizza the hot dry peppers with their yellow seeds serve to spice a soft cheese. For an example turn to the recipe on page 61.

Nutmeg, It. *noce moscata*, is the seed of a tree for which the Latin name is *myristica fragrens*. This sweet aromatic spice is used in Italian dishes where spinach and soft cheeses play important roles, like the *Genoese* tarts which appear at the end of this book (see pages 148 to 151). The spice is also used in béchamels destined to cover lasagne and also in some recipes for ragu' and meat-based pasta sauce. Nutmeg should be freshly scraped as the powdered variety sold in packets quickly loses its flavour.

PIZZA
ALLA
NAPOLETANA

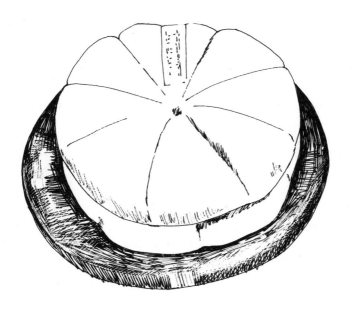

PIZZA ALLA NAPOLETANA
NAPLES AND
CLASSIC NEAPOLITAN PIZZA

To me, a *pizza alla Napoletana* sums up the joyousness of Naples; it is as round and red as the southern sun, as robust and salty as the city's history and as perfumed and smooth as the manners of its citizens. And the ingredients, dark ripe tomatoes, strong crust, salty anchovies, scented oregano and smooth mozzarella, are cooked in the roaring heat of miniature Vesuvian volcanoes, the tiny beehive-shaped ovens that in *pizzerie*, large and small, are dotted all over the shrill, passionate streets of the city.

Naples, first a Greek city then Roman, was, the Neapolitans insist, the birthplace of pizza and witness of its forebear, a simple flat bread eaten with a relish, a piquant accompaniment. In Pompeii, victim of Vesuvius, the Street of Abundance, dug from the preserving ash, reveals a life of plenty. Prosperous bakers like Publius Paquius Proculus made fortunes from supplying fine loaves to the townspeople. And fine loaves they were, made from hard wheat, their surface scored into petals so that they could be easily divided and, sometimes, elegant inscriptions were pressed in a long narrow row into the dough. And sad loaves they are those destined not to be eaten, baked on August 24th, 79 A.D. and carbonized by the great eruption.

Naples today is a magnificent rakish ruin, a raddled overblown beauty. The immense Bourbon and Savoyard buildings are cracked and stained, the *Gallerie*, those splendid late 19th-century arcades, are in want of panes of glass and the dozens of opera houses are boarded over, their robust curvacious decoration host to weeds. But her streets are still full of life and gaiety, the *napoletanità* that enchanted so many 18th and 19th-century travellers. Campania, her fertile countryside, still provides the rich produce that delighted Goethe. The pastry shops are full of delicate *sfogliatelle*, light flaky pastries, fat *torte rustici*, four inches deep, rich with soft cheese, studded with prosciutto. Real mozzarella is still to be found in cheese shops of stunning quality. The *frutti di mare* has an incomparable flavour and the tomatoes are deeper in colour and flavour than any other.

The narrow *vicoli* off the main streets are canyon-like, the tall houses throw blue shadows on to the stucco walls and each house has a large shrine dedicated to the Virgin cut into its walls, just as in Pompeii there were shrines dedicated to Isis. At each shrine there are flowers, perhaps magnificent bunches of tall yellow tiger lilies placed with reverent abandon in glass vases on each side of the painting. In streets like these you will find small, almost decrepit *pizzerie* decked out with bright tablecloths, vases of artificial and fresh flowers, religious pictures, and turn of the century photographs of the proprietor's great grandparents. In the corner will be the glowing oven, shaped like an oversized beehive and covered with small but thick, oblong tiles, perhaps wasp-yellow and black alternated in a simple chequered pattern. It will be attended by the *pizzaiolo* and his assistant who are always men. And around the doorway there will be hand-written signs advertising *Pizza Napoletana*, *Pizza Margherita* and *Pizza Marinara*, the classic *pizze* that were sold in 19th-century Naples, which are held in near reverence by Neapolitans and have travelled all over the world. These classic *pizze* are invariably to be found on the menus of all Italian *pizzerie*.

Pizza alla Napoletana

tomato pulp
mozzarella
anchovies
oregano
olive oil
lard

This is the *benjamino*, the favourite, the pizza that is the essence of all *pizze*. To make it as ardent as it should be, the tomatoes must be rich and ripe and the olive oil strong and fruity. Note the recipe for *Polpa di Pomodoro* on page 52.

To make this pizza you will need sufficient dough for one medium-size pizza, made according to the instructions on page 29; a small piece of lard the size of a walnut; 3 tablespoons of olive oil; 8 oz/1 cup/ 240 g of ripe tomato pulp (see page 52); 3 oz/½ cup/80 g of mozzarella cut into small dice; 4 anchovy fillets; salt and black pepper; a large pinch of the most fragrant oregano that you can muster. Oven temperature: 425°F/220°C/7.

Roll out the dough into a circle and place it to prove or rise on an oiled flat pizza tin or floured board if you wish to bake on tiles. Heat the oven to the required temperature. Rub the nut of lard over the proved dough to add its particular flavour, then smear on one tablespoon of the olive oil. Add the tomato pulp, spreading it over evenly but leaving a border of about half an inch round the edge. Sprinkle on the mozzarella, arrange here and there the anchovy fillets, broken into pieces, add a very little salt and pepper, and abundant oregano, and finally dribble on the rest of the olive oil.

Put the pizza into the hot oven and bake it for twenty minutes until the crust is golden and the cheese bubbles. Serve it with a great deal of strong red wine and enjoy it.

Pizza Margherita

tomato pulp
mozzarella
basil
olive oil

Pizza Margherita, always to be found on the menu of any pizzeria, was named in 1889 in honour of Queen Margherita of Savoy and its colours are those of the *bandiera*, the Italian flag, green, white and red. It is made with one of the simplest but most effective combinations of flavours. The ripe tomato melds beautifully with soft creamy mozzarella made from water buffalo milk, and the cool green fragrant basil perfectly compliments the tomatoes' sweet acidity.

To make a Pizza Margherita *you will need sufficient dough for one medium-size pizza made according to the instructions on page 29; 8 oz/1 cup/240 g of ripe tomato pulp (see page 52); 4 oz/¾ cup/100 g of mozzarella; salt; 6 or 7 fresh basil leaves; 2 tablespoons of the best* extra vergine *olive oil that you can obtain. Oven temperature: 425°F/220°C/7.*

Have your oven heating, while you roll out the dough into a circle. Let the dough prove or rise for ten to fifteen minutes on an oiled tin or floured board. Spread the tomato on the proved dough leaving a small border around the edge, then lay on the mozzarella cut into thin slices. Scatter on a little salt then two or three of the basil leaves, and lastly sprinkle on the two tablespoons of olive oil. Bake the pizza for twenty minutes. Before you take it to the table scatter on the remaining basil leaves as the cooked ones will have become brown in the heat of the oven.

Pizza Marinara
Pizza with Tomatoes and Garlic

The pizza *Marinara* is a very simple form of pizza but is no less delicious for that simplicity. It consists of a layer of ripe tomato and a great deal of fresh garlic skinned and cut into thick slivers. The garlic, which must be crisp and fresh, will add a pungent almost throat-burning excitement to the flavour. So this pizza is best made when the new season's garlic, plump and purple-skinned, reaches the markets.

tomatoes
garlic
olive oil

To make a Pizza Marinara *you will need sufficient dough for one medium-size pizza base made according to the instructions on page 29; 8 oz/1 cup/240 g of ripe tomatoes, skinned, seeded, chopped and drained; 3 plump cloves of garlic cut into slices, salt, pepper and about 2 tablespoons of green olive oil. Oven temperature: 425°F/220°C/7.*

Have your oven heating with your baking stone or tiles heating within it. Make the dough base, rolling out or pushing the dough into a circle and leaving the edges slightly thicker than the middle. Slide the dough on to a floured board or place it in an oiled pizza tin. Let it prove or rise while the oven becomes hot.

Spread on the tomato, making sure that it is not watery, sprinkle the sliced garlic here and there, add salt and black pepper, then a final drizzle of oil. Let it bake for about twenty minutes until the edge of the crust, the *cornicione*, is swollen and golden. Bring it to the table immediately and serve it with more olive oil dribbled on top, and perhaps an *insalata verde* to be eaten afterwards and some fierce red wine.

Pizza Bianca

mozzarella
anchovies
basil
pecorino or
   parmesan
olive oil

Pizza can also be made *in bianca*, that is without any layer of ripe tomato, and the very earliest versions of pizza were certainly made in this fashion because in general tomatoes were a late addition to the Italian kitchen, and although they were cultivated and used in the south of Italy early in the last century it was not until towards the end of the 19th century that they were introduced all over the New Italy.

In the mid-1800s the most common type of pizza sold in Naples was simply flavoured with oil and garlic, to which *cecinielli*, tiny larval anchovies and sardines, were sometimes added. These tiny fish are now not commonly used and their place has been taken by anchovies, either preserved in salt or under olive oil. The popular 19th-century herbs were oregano and basil as they still are today. Basil was used frequently to perfume pizza seasoned with grated cheese. Lard was used as an unguent as well as olive oil and more extravagent *pizze* held *prosciutto*, mozzarella, clams and tomatoes, but the poorer you were the plainer was your pizza.

To make a Pizza Bianca *you will need sufficient dough to make a medium-size pizza base made from the recipe on page 29; 6 oz/1 cup/ 170 g of mozzarella; 3 or 4 anchovy fillets; 6 or 7 fresh basil leaves; salt and freshly ground black pepper; 2 tablespoons of good strong olive oil; 2 tablespoons of grated pecorino cheese, or parmesan if pecorino is not available (for information about Italian cheeses and their alternatives, see page 54). Oven temperature: 425°F/220°C/7.*

Have your oven heating while you roll out the circle of dough and let it prove or rise on an oiled pizza tin or a floured card or board. Meanwhile cut up the mozzarella into dice and split the anchovy fillets into several pieces.

When the oven is hot start to dress the pizza. Add the pieces of anchovy to the mozzarella and toss them together briefly, then spread the mixture on to the circle of dough being careful to leave a small border. Strew on a few of the basil leaves, leaving some aside. Add a very little salt, as the anchovy will provide its own supply, and a little black pepper. Pour the olive oil in a thin stream over the surface and finally sprinkle on the grated pecorino or parmesan.

Bake the pizza for twenty minutes until the crust is golden. Just before taking the pizza to the table, add the rest of the basil leaves to give a fresh taste and a note of colour.

Quattro Stagione
Four Seasons

tomato pulp
mozzarella
prosciutto
button
  mushrooms
artichoke hearts
capers
anchovies
olive oil

The *Quattro Stagione* is an elaboration on the old-fashioned *pizze* sold in the streets of Naples where the dough was still the most important part of the dish and the seasonings played a minor and more economical role. It is a good example of an ancient and simple food which has adapted to the needs of society without losing its basic good quality. *Pizze* of this type loaded with succulent ingredients are the answer to the demand for a one-dish meal. Customers at Italy's countless *pizzerie* want a little more than the original slice of flat bread spread with a little oil, salt, and a few slivers of garlic. A perfect snack for a cold morning, but one that does not stand up to an evening's entertainment of friends sitting around talking, drinking wine and eating a simple meal.

Today the emphasis lies more on the fillings than the crust. In fact in Italy the old-fashioned pizza crust, which was thick and cake-like, although still to be found in Neapolitan *pizzerie*, has in other cities given way to a thinner crisper crust; due perhaps to the new Italian love affair with lighter healthier foods.

The fillings of a *Quattro Stagione*, the four quarters divided by small strips of dough or four anchovy fillets, have contrasting tastes and textures. Arranged upon a bed of tomato there can be *prosciutto*, sliced mushrooms, perhaps preserved artichoke hearts, a little mozzarella, a few olives. However, a pizza *Quattro Stagione* is not an excuse to use up any old oddments that may be expiring in the refrigerator; the ingredients should work well together in texture and taste and everything should be as fresh as possible when using vegetables and of good quality when using bottled or preserved products such as artichoke hearts, capers or olives.

To make a pizza Quattro Stagione *you will need sufficient dough to make a medium-size pizza base as given in the recipe on page 29; 8 oz/1 cup/240 g of tomato pulp (see page 52); 4 oz/³⁄₄ cup/100 g of mozzarella; 2 thin slices of* prosciutto; *1 oz/¹⁄₂ cup/25 g of raw button mushrooms, finely sliced; 2 or 3 preserved artichoke hearts; a few capers; 1 or 2 anchovy fillets; 2 tablespoons of olive oil; salt. Oven temperature: 425°F/220°C/7.*

Prepare your disc of dough, reserving a little for the dividing strips. Lay the disc to prove or rise on an oiled flat pizza tin. When the oven is fully heated, dress the dough with a layer of tomato pulp and a little of the mozzarella.

Divide the disc into four quarters with small twists of the reserved dough. In each quarter of the disc arrange the other ingredients. In one, place the *prosciutto* cut into wide ribbons, in another the finely sliced mushrooms, in the third the artichokes, drained and halved if they are large. Finally, in the fourth place the rest of the mozzarella, a few capers and an anchovy or two.

Pour over the pizza a small stream of olive oil, making sure that a sufficient quantity goes over the mushrooms, which will need the moisture. When you have sprinkled on a little salt place the pizza in the hot oven and bake it for twenty minutes.

Of course you may want to vary the diverse fillings, using perhaps some red bell peppers cut into strips and gently cooked in olive oil, maybe a little *salame* or piquant sausage, or perhaps a few wild mushrooms if they are available.

Pizza con Olio e Aglio
Pizza with Olive Oil and Garlic

garlic
olive oil

In most *pizzerie* it is possible to order a plain pizza, a simple circle of baked dough, to accompany a steak instead of ordinary table bread, but there is no reason why one should not revive the original *Pizza coll Oglio e Aglio* of mid-19th-century Naples.

To make this simple dish of 4 to 5 small pizze *you will need* all *the dough from the recipe on page 29; 2 or 3 cloves of fresh crisp garlic; salt; 3 to 4 tablespoons of excellent fruity* extra vergine *olive oil. The perfume of the olive oil will be enhanced by the heat of the pizza.*

Divide the dough into four or five portions, flatten these into rough circles, and let them prove or rise on a floured work surface. Cut the cloves of garlic into thin slivers and press them here and there over the surfaces of the *pizze*.

Meanwhile, heat your grill or broiler up to its absolute maximum. Put two or three of the circles of dough on to the rack in the pan, placing them as near to the heat as possible. Let them whiten, take the pan away and turn the *pizze* over; repeat this step once more and let the dough start to burn in small round patches. When the *pizze* are cooked, which will take about three minutes a side in all, put them on a warm plate, sprinkle them with salt and trickle the oil over each one. Take them to the table immediately.

Serve these small *pizze* with a fresh tomato soup, a dish of *prosciutto* and *salame* or a cheese- and parsley-flavoured *frittata*, Italian omelette.

Basil, olives and Silvana's olive oil

Marjoram and melanzane on a blue plate

I POMODORI
TOMATOES

In late August, kitchen tables all over Italy are covered with piles of glossy scarlet tomatoes. The fruit is at its ripest and this is the best time to bottle it, to make *pomaruola* (tomato pulp flavoured with a little onion, carrot and basil) and *concentrato di pomodoro*, the tomato concentrate that we buy in tubes. These conserves will last the careful Italian housewife all year long for her pasta sauces.

Silvana, my neighbour, always has a cupboard full of glass preserving jars brimful with plum tomatoes flavoured with fresh basil leaves. She preserves so many tomatoes that the floors of her storeroom are carpeted in the red fruit at the right season.

In the hotter south of Italy at this time you will see enormous shallow pottery bowls of tomato paste left to dry in the sun, the surfaces thickly encrusted with salt. This coarse salt protects the tomato paste from dust and also serves to draw out excess water. The paste becomes rich and concentrated, and has the inimitable sweetness of vine-ripened fruit.

Tomatoes were brought to Europe from South America by the Spanish in the 16th century and there is a legend that the first seeds to arrive in Italy were brought to Naples by Neapolitan sailors. Italians, being cautious about new foods, first used tomato plants as decorations and a poor opinion prevailed of their flavour and culinary use. The naturalist Castor Durante in his *Herbario Nuovo* published in 1584 had this to say of them: 'One eats the tomato in the same way as the aubergine, with pepper, salt and oil, but they give scarce and poor nutriment.' In 1607 Francesco Angelita, a native of the Marche region of Italy, wrote a treatise on the nature of and ways of cultivating the tomato or the *pomi d'oro* as it was called. However, the first recipe now known for tomato sauce was given by a Jesuit priest-cook, Padre Francesco Gaudentio, in his book *Il Panunto Toscano* published in Rome in 1705. I do not think this recipe is generally known outside Italy, except perhaps by enthusiasts of culinary history.

> Manner of cooking the *pomi d'oro*. This fruit is very similar to the apple, they are cultivated in the garden and are cooked in the following way. Take the tomatoes, cut them into pieces, put them in a pan with oil, salt, chopped garlic and wild savory. Let them cook turning them frequently and if you like add a few soft breadcrumbs.

This simple recipe is, in essence, almost exactly the same as modern recipes for tomato sauces.

By the end of the 18th century elaborate and dainty dishes were being made with tomatoes in the Naples that delighted Goethe with the richness of her markets. At that time one of Italy's great cooks was pleasing guests with dishes of great delicacy. Casanova, Sir William Hamilton and his flighty wife, Emma, enjoyed these banquets. The cook, eventually to become prelate, was called Vincenzo Corrado, and he was the presiding genius of the kitchens of the Palazzo Francavilla. In 1773 he published the first of many editions of *Il Cuoco Galante*, The Gallant Cook. The subtle recipes he invented, using fresh produce served with light *coulis* of tomatoes or shellfish, were to my mind two hundred years in advance of *cuisine nouvelle*. Corrado also went into great and delicious detail about the preparation of the tomato.

First, he remarks that: 'Tomatoes are pleasing. To serve them they must first be turned on the grill or left for a little time in boiling water to remove their skins. Then one must cut them in half and take out the seeds.' Among his imaginative recipes there is one for *pomodori salpiconati*, tomatoes stuffed with sweetbreads that have first been cooked in butter, herbs and spices. Another suggests filling the tomatoes with chopped parsley, onion, rocket (arugula), tarragon and mint mixed with egg yolk and provolone, frying them then serving them with a *coulis* of *prosciutto*. Again, tomatoes could be stuffed with parmesan, parsley and spices bound with egg, then floured and fried until they were golden globes and served with more parmesan and butter. They could also be stuffed with herb-scented fish and served with a *coulis* of prawns or large shrimps. He also confected a most elegant and dainty *budin* with crushed tomato pulp, cream, parmesan, soft breadcrumbs and cinnamon, all mixed into a thick cream and baked in a buttered dish.

Corrado gives too a recipe for *pomodoro alla Napoletana*: halved tomato shells filled with anchovies, oregano, garlic, parsley and breadcrumbs, baked in the oven. A great many of these ingredients found their way on to the classic *pizza alla Napoletana*.

The tomato had 'arrived' to revolutionize Italian cooking. However it was not until quite late in the 19th century that the jolly red tide swept all over the peninsula, carried by the unifying army of Garibaldi.

Possibly it was because of the splendidly suitable climate that the tomato clung so tenaciously to Naples. In fact in an English gardening book written in 1885 it says that 'it is only in the south of Europe that the tomato can be perfectly grown without the aid of artificial heat'. Today, I would be tempted to agree with this sentiment if the sentence ended with the word 'grown'. In southern Italy they cultivate flavourful varieties of tomato like San Marzano and Lampadina as well as the plump fleshy Marmandes. There the sun is strong enough to ripen the fruit on the vine and their taste, as a consequence, is superb. They can be skinned and used in raw juicy segments on pizza, as is traditional, without any preparation.

The sun is not so vivid in our northern countries so tomatoes need to be carefully chosen and given a little help before they will add much flavour to a pizza. Grow your own Marmande or plum tomatoes if you can, or buy these varieties, making sure that they are not soft and watery. Avoid the round, insipid, supermarket tomato that is as tasteless as it is spherical. These tomatoes and the sauces made from them are usually bitter and metallic.

When in the depths of winter and at other times when tomatoes are expensive, buy, as do all Italians, canned plum tomatoes, but make sure they are produced in Italy. Pizza is a simple thing, and it does not make sense to spend a great deal on expensive fresh tomatoes to make what is traditionally an economical dish for feeding hungry families, when a good inexpensive alternative can be found.

As the tomato stars in a great many pizza seasonings, I have in this section included just three recipes. One for tomato pulp to go on top of the pizza, one for a fresh-tasting tomato sauce to pour over baked *calzoni* (see page 99) and one for a pizza using fresh sliced tomatoes and *extra vergine* olive oil. However, for the tomato lover, *Pizza alla Napoletana* on page 44, *Pizza Marinara* on page 45, *Pizza Rosa* on page 98 and the *Caccione* invented by Valentino Caldiero, as well as his *Pizza al Noci* on page 115, employ the delicious fruit to advantage.

Polpa di Pomodoro
Tomato Pulp

tomatoes
garlic
olive oil

Italian canned tomatoes and also fresh ones can be improved quite simply to make a satisfactory juicy seasoning, and the following recipe will yield enough tomato to cover a medium-size pizza. The tomato flavour is concentrated and enhanced by the olive oil.

You will need 2 tablespoons of flavourful green olive oil, 1 clove of garlic crushed and chopped; 2 or 3 turns from the black pepper mill; 14 oz/400 g can of Italian peeled plum tomatoes, or 16 oz/450 g of fresh ripe tomatoes deprived of their skins and hard sections and cut into segments. Lastly, a pinch of salt.

Take a heavy saucepan and in it warm the olive oil over a low heat, then add the chopped garlic and the black pepper. Their purpose is to perfume the oil. Watch the hissing garlic with care to see that is does not brown, as this would alter the flavour of the pulp, which must be fresh-tasting.

After a scarce minute add the can of tomatoes or the chopped fresh ones. Stir the mixture around with a wooden fork to break up the tomatoes evenly. Add the pinch of salt. Now raise the heat a little and let the mixture cook until the liquid has reduced and you are left with a dense thick pulp.

As a rough guide, after about six or seven minutes of cooking a 14 oz/400 g can (which will contain about 12 oz/350 g of tomatoes) will reduce to about 8 oz/1 cup/240 g of thick pulp. The cooking time for fresh tomatoes will depend on their juiciness.

Salsa di Pomodoro
Tomato Sauce

tomatoes
garlic
basil
olive oil

This recipe is very like that written by Padre Francesco in the year 1705 (see page 49). This cool perfumed sauce is excellent when poured over the hot crisp crust of a *calzone*.

You will need 3 tablespoons of fruity green olive oil; 2 cloves of garlic crushed and chopped; black pepper; one 14 oz/400 g can of Italian San Marzano *peeled tomatoes, or 1 lb/450 g of fresh ripe tomatoes deprived of their skins and hard parts and then cut into segments; ½ teaspoon of salt; 5 of the giant variety of basil leaves or 10 normal ones.*

Take a heavy saucepan and in it heat the olive oil over a low heat, then add the chopped garlic and a spray of black pepper. Make sure that the garlic does not brown. After a scarce minute add the tomato, and stir the mixture with a wooden spoon to break up the pulp evenly. Add the salt and let the tomato stew for six to seven minutes over a gentle heat; you do not want to reduce the mixture as for *Polpa di Pomodoro*.

Wipe the basil leaves but do not wash them as this would only dissipate their perfume. Add them whole to the sauce and cook gently until the fresh tomato is soft and the basil has given up its flavour. Before serving the sauce allow it to cool and remove the basil leaves, which will now be dark and wilted.

Pizza col Pomodoro Crudo e Basilico
Pizza with Raw Tomato and Basil

This is a delicious pizza to be made at the height of summer when tomatoes are ripe and basil flourishes.

tomato
basil
olive oil

To make the usual medium-size round pizza you will need sufficient dough (see page 29); 1 large or 2 small Marmande tomatoes; 4 tablespoons of the very best extra vergine *olive oil; coarse salt and freshly ground black pepper; a handful of basil leaves. Oven temperature: 425°F/220°C/7.*

Have the oven heating while you roll out the dough into a circle and lay it to prove or rise on an oiled pizza tin, or on a card or peel if you are going to cook on tiles or a bakestone. Slice the tomatoes into slim rounds and cut away the hard stem part.

When the oven is hot simply lay the tomato slices on the dough, sprinkle on a little coarse salt and two tablespoons of the olive oil. Put the pizza on an upper-middle shelf of the oven and let it cook for twenty minutes until the crust is golden.

Just before taking the pizza to the table dribble on the remaining two tablespoons of olive oil, a spray of black pepper, and arrange the basil leaves here and there over the tomatoes.

Cold *extra vergine* olive oil, when poured over a hot pizza crust, gives the baked dough a soft creamy flavour which is quite delicious.

IL FORMAGGIO
CHEESE

The art of cheese making in Italy is an ancient one – it was the Etruscans who invented the forefather of parmesan. Cato, Varro and Columella are founts of information on the subject and Roman gourmets enjoyed aged cheeses both plain and smoked as well as fresh cheeses and yoghurts. The first time that gorgonzola is mentioned in the annals of its eponymous tiny birthplace is in 879 A.D. But not only is the activity ancient, the variety of modern Italian cheeses is immense.

One of the pleasures of food shopping in Italy is to stand before a cheese counter and select some from the great variety on display; perhaps to serve with fruit at the end of an evening meal or perhaps as part of the main dish. Of the vast array of cheeses that are to be bought and enjoyed in Italy five appear frequently in recipes for *pizze*, breads and tarts: mozzarella, parmesan, pecorino, gorgonzola and fontina.

MOZZARELLA

Mozzarella cheese, a most important ingredient in many *pizze*, comes originally from the south of Italy and is immensely popular in Campania and Naples where it is used abundantly in Neapolitan cuisine, and where they are fortunate in still being able to buy the genuine article. As you will see from the recipes in this book mozzarella is one of the main ingredients of Neapolitan pizza due to its flavour, its creaminess and the ease with which it melts in the oven without becoming hard and rubbery.

Real mozzarella is made from the milk of water buffaloes, ungainly black beasts with horns that lie flat across their skulls like ossified permanent waves before branching out into generous curlicues. The water buffalo or *gamoose* as it is called in Egypt is fond of wallowing in mud and is kept by the southerners especially for its rich, high fat, wholesome milk. The curds obtained from the milk are dried, treated with boiling water, and cut into strips which are then torn up and pressed back together again so that the cheese is formed of many layers, *pasta filata*. It is pulled and twisted into various shapes and sizes, some like skeins of wool, others round like oranges.

Mozzarella is eaten fresh. It does not keep for more than two weeks, and in the south it is usually sold from deep dishes in which the cheeses lie in their own whey, and in this manner they keep a moist surface.

Buffalo milk mozzarella is a chalky white colour, but the type of mozzarella that is commonly available all over Italy is made from cow's milk and should properly be called *fior di latte*. It has a creamy ivory colour, is blander in taste and does not have the particular lactic savour of the real water buffalo product. In fact, most mozzarella used in Italian cooking today is made from cow's milk and is manufactured all over Italy. Real mozzarella is a treasure hard to find outside the south.

In April 1986, a new law came into force in Italy regarding mozzarella, which will present some manufacturers with problems. In future the ingredients of the cheese, plus the date after which it will begin to deteriorate, the *dato di scadenza*, will have to be printed on the outside of the package. A great deal of *mozzarella di bufala* sold in the south does not come in packages but is sold from tubs of whey, so new labelling will be required. Some of the alleged *mozzarella di bufala* which is sold in packages is made from a mixture of cow and buffalo milk. Some which is sold as the genuine article contains only cow's milk and unfortunately the worst sort is made completely from powdered milk and chemicals. Happily for the Italians, and for those of us who buy imported mozzarella, this new law will mean that we will know exactly what we are buying and the reputation of genuine mozzarella will be safeguarded against petty frauds. What is jokingly called the new D.O.C. mozzarella after the wine classification could become a source of great pride and prove to be a renaissance of a fine product.

As well as going into such dishes as *parmigiana di melanzane* or *parmigiano di peperoncini* or *zucchini*, mozzarella can be used to make such things as *palline di mozzarella*, which are little balls made of the cheese worked into a paste and mixed with various seasonings such as chopped parsley, *prosciutto*, parmesan, salt and pepper, then deep-fried in hot oil. Of course mozzarella forms the chief ingredient of the simple and cooling summer dish *caprese* which consists of rounds of fresh white cheese topped with a slice of ripe tomato and a leaf or two of basil, the whole dressed with a liberal stream of the best Tuscan olive oil.

PARMIGIANO
Parmigiano is used in pizza not so much as the body of the seasoning as is mozzarella, but more in the way of adding an extra depth, a richer note to the general flavour. Its taste becomes stronger, more insistent when heated. It plays an important role in a *Pizza ai Quattro Formaggi* (see page 59) and is also delicious on a *Pizza Bianca* (see page 46) when there is no pecorino to be had.

A piece of *grana*, preferably *Parmigiano Reggiano*, is indispensable in an Italian pantry because of its incomparable flavour and its versatility. To me *Reggiano* has a deeper richer flavour than *Grana Padana*, its close neighbour, though it too has much to commend it and its sweeter milkier flavour goes well in delicate dishes. However, the majesty of a well-aged *Parmigiano Reggiano*, eaten in walnut-sized pieces, and accompanied by a good heavy Italian red wine such as an old *Brunello* or a *Vin Nobile di Montepulciano*, has no rivals. To properly enjoy the crystalline texture of parmesan you must break off lumps with the aid of the small diamond-shaped blade of a parmesan knife; to cut thin slices is to miss some of the pleasure. It was, some years ago, and possibly still is in some circles today, considered vulgar to eat parmesan as a dessert cheese. I do not know the reason for this nicety of behaviour but I do most positively side with the vulgarians on this point.

Parmesan goes into the most luxurious Italian dishes such as *parmigiano tartufato*, which is a dish of alternating layers of truffles and parmesan baked in the oven, and the justly famed *melanzane parmigiana*, layers of aubergine (eggplant) and parmesan similarly baked, and it is also used, again with truffles, as a stuffing for roast pheasant. On the other hand, *parmigiano* can also enrich the simplest of vegetable soups, serves as an addition to countless pasta dishes, is used in the filling of *agnolotti* and *tortellini*, and is superb and comes entirely into its own when eaten sprinkled over a plain risotto or a plate of home-made *tagliatelle*. It also, as I have said, lends distinction to many pizza seasonings.

PECORINO

Another hard cheese, this time made in the regions of Tuscany and also around Umbria and Lazio is pecorino, also called *cacio* or *caciotta* in Tuscany where it is traditionally made in small forms of a kilo (two pounds) or less. It is an excellent cheese for grating and is used in many regional dishes like *torte rustici* and *focacce* to give a country flavour of great character. Around Rome it is called *pecorino romana* and is made in big wheels weighing anything from about eight to twenty kilos each. The Roman cheese is sharper and stronger than the Tuscan variety. In Sardinia, which is famous for its skilled shepherds, the cheese is called *sardo* and is made by the shepherds themselves.

In fact, genuine pecorino made from ewe's milk is becoming hard to find and the mass-produced kind made in small factories and dairies is frequently made from pasturized cow's milk mixed with some ewe's milk, also pasturized, which of course radically alters the flavour – and for the worse. I buy my pecorino, when we happen to be in the area, from a family of Sardinians who keep their flocks grazing within sight of the beautiful church called the *Tempietto di San Biagio* at Montepulciano, and their cheese is excellent. Sardinian shepherds are often pleased to take up residence in Tuscany where they can pasture their sheep within living distance of their families. In Sardinia they have to live away from their villages, travelling miles into the mountains to good pastures.

One of the best places to find good pecorino is on the market stalls of small Umbrian and Tuscan country towns where the stallholder may still buy his supplies from the farmers' wives who continue to make the cheese in the old manner. Pecorino is sold in two conditions: fresh, which is creamy-white and soft, and mature, in which case the small round forms of cheese have been kept and regularly turned until they have developed a hard yellow crust and the interior is golden and sharp-tasting. Mature pecorino which has been kept, anointed with olive oil and wrapped in almond leaves, is a rare treat when eaten with a sweet pear at the end of a meal.

GORGONZOLA

Another delicious and useful cheese is gorgonzola. Today this is made all over Lombardy but was originally named after the town of its birth, Gorgonzola, with its nearby cool caves in which the cheese was made and stored. These caves held within them the mould that gave the cheese its characteristic blue-green veins. Today the mould is induced with the addition of penicillin moulds to the curd. The cheese is made from rich cow's milk and has a high fat content, giving a soft, luscious creamy texture.

Good quality genuine *gorgonzola a due paste* is made in layers of cold and hot curd. The difference in temperature between the layers leaves a tiny gap in which the characteristic naturally occurring mould flourishes in the trapped air. Ordinary commercial gorgonzola employs doses of mould which also cannot live without air; to furnish this the cheese is pierced at regular intervals with wires that leave a tiny air passage. These lines can be seen quite easily running through a slice of the cheese. The surprising and enjoyable quality of gorgonzola is that although it has a special piquant flavour it is never harsh. Gorgonzola is sold in two different types, *dolce* and *piccante*, sweet (that is mild) and sharp. The younger cheeses are sweeter. Actually gorgonzola is but one among a type of cheese called *stracchino*, which is again a soft, fresh, high fat cow's milk cheese usually enjoyed as a dessert but also used in savoury *torte*.

Apart from it being a good dessert cheese, gorgonzola happily flavours *risotti, pasta* and *crespelle*, and responds well to being baked on top of a pizza, whether as part of a *Pizza ai Quattro Formaggi* or simply paired with mozzarella. It is also sometimes added fresh to a baked pizza before it is taken to the table. Its flavour is inclined to soften when heated.

FONTINA

Genuine fontina is made in the Val d'Aosta, the long mountainous valley leading out of north-western Italy, and, properly, is made from the whole milk of Valdostana cows. However, imitation fontina is produced in other parts of Italy and in other European countries; in my local shop they have fontina from Holland and also from Germany. It is a smooth waxy-textured cheese, mild when young but becoming stronger with age. It is *the* cheese for making *fonduta*, that incredibly smooth silken fondue, exceptionally good examples of which I have eaten in old traditional *Torinese* restaurants. Fontina is the fourth cheese which makes up the classic combination of *I Quattro Formaggi* (page 59), the other three being gorgonzola, mozzarella and *parmigiano*. The melted flavours of these four very different though complementary cheeses go into the splendid *risotto ai quattro formaggi* and the pizza of the same name. Fontina and mozzarella are splendid cooking cheeses, they melt superbly and smoothly and do not become hard and rubbery. They form the body of the sauce; the fontina soft and mellow, the mozzarella faintly lactic and sharp. Parmesan adds a deeper richer note and gorgonzola has its own distinction.

When buying cheeses, select the best quality that you are able to afford. Do not be fobbed off with factory-made industrialized cheeses with flavours as plastic as their wrappings. Try and buy your mozzarella from an Italian delicatessen and read its label carefully. Ask the Italian proprietor for his advice as to which mozzarella is best and which grade of parmesan he eats; if he has no pecorino, encourage him to stock it.

A new generation of cheesemakers has sprung up in both Britain and the United States, making delicious and genuine cheeses. Experiment with them, remembering the basic rules – some cheeses must respond well to heat and form a smooth body, others must add rich or piquant notes to the general flavour. This is how recipes develop and grow.

Pizza ai Quattro Formaggi
Pizza with Four Cheeses

For a medium-size pizza you will need sufficient dough from the recipe on page 29; about 2 oz/a little less than ½ cup/50 g each of mozzarella, fontina and gorgonzola, all diced into small pieces, and the same amount of parmesan, freshly grated through the large holes in the grater; 2 tablespoons of olive oil; a little salt and a generous spray of freshly ground black pepper. Oven temperature: 425°F/220°C/7.

mozzarella
gorgonzola
fontina
parmesan
olive oil

While the oven is heating, roll out the dough into a circle, and leave it to rest either on a lightly oiled tin or floured card for the tile method of baking.

When the oven is ready, dress the pizza. First smear some of the olive oil over the surface of the dough, to encourage the cheese to meld in with the base. Next sprinkle on the pieces of cheese, mixing them up together, then dust them all over with the grated parmesan and add a little salt and a spray of pepper. Finally dribble on the remaining olive oil.

Put the pizza in the oven, either in its tin or by sliding it off the card or peel on to the hot tiles. Let it cook for about twenty minutes on a middle shelf until the crust is golden. If the pizza seems to be cooking too fast and the topping is in danger of drying out, you can always turn down the temperature a little after about twelve minutes.

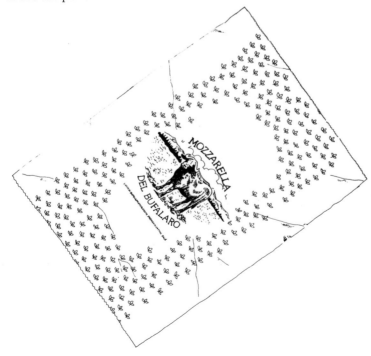

Pizza con La Mozzarella e Polpa d'Oliva
Pizza with Mozzarella and Crushed Olives

mozzarella
olive pulp
oregano
olive oil

Olives are sold in Italy in great profusion of size, colour and fla-vour. Some can be obtained soaked in olive oil seasoned with thyme or oregano, these are called *olive condite*; others are sold sweet, dry and wrinkled; green olives usually come in brine and the richest most nutritious olives are those that are hand- picked when they have achieved that strange greeny-purple hue, the stage of ripening before they have become completely mature and black. Hand-picked purple olives make the best olive oil and now very often they may be found in another form, that of *Polpa d'Oliva*, a paste of crushed olives (see page 35).

To make this pizza you will need sufficient dough for one medium-size pizza base as given in the recipe on page 29; 6 oz/1 cup/170 g of mozzarella; 3 tablespoons of olive pulp (see page 35); a very little salt and a generous amount of black pepper; a pinch of oregano; 3 tables-poons of olive oil. Oven temperature: 425°F/220°C/7.

Have your oven heating while you roll out the dough into a circle. Let it prove on a floured board or oiled pizza tin.

Meanwhile cut up the mozzarella into small dice and put them into a bowl. Mix the olive pulp into the diced mozzarella so that it is evenly spread through; if the paste is on the dry side moisten it with a little extra olive oil. Next, spread this mixture on the pizza, sprinkle on a hint of salt and a deal more black pepper, scatter over the oregano and finally sprinkle on the olive oil. Put the pizza in the hot oven where it will take about twenty minutes to bake.

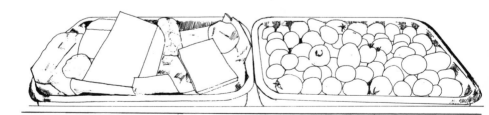

Pizza con Il Gorgonzola
Pizza with Gorgonzola

To make a medium-size round pizza you will need sufficient dough made from the recipe on page 29; 6 oz/1 cup/170 g of mild gorgonzola cheese; 10 walnuts broken up into small pieces; 3 tablespoons of good olive oil. Oven temperature: 425°F/220°C/7.

**gorgonzola
walnuts
olive oil**

Roll out your circle of dough and let it prove on the oiled pizza tin or floured board while the oven is heating up. When the oven is hot smear about 1 tablespoon of the olive oil over the surface of the dough. Next cut up the gorgonzola into small pieces and spread them on top. Finally scatter on the walnuts and the rest of the olive oil. Consign it to the hot oven and bake for about twenty minutes or until the crust is golden.

This recipe also makes very good *pizzette*, and I would suggest that a large pizza should be divided into triangles and served in small portions, as a whole pizza for each person with this rich covering would be too much. If the gorgonzola at your disposal is sharp, reduce the quantity and mix it with a little mozzarella. Never use Danish Blue as a substitute as it is too harsh.

Pizza Piccante
Spiced Pizza

To make a medium-size round pizza you will need, besides sufficient dough made with the recipe on page 29, about 3 oz/½ cup/80 g of diced mozzarella cheese; 3 oz/½ cup/80 g of freshly grated fontina, provolone or parmesan; 2 tablespoons of olive oil; 1 dried red chilli pepper cut into small pieces; a little salt. Oven temperature: 425°F/220°C/7.

**mozzarella
fontina or
   provolone or
   parmesan
chilli pepper
olive oil**

While the oven is heating up roll out the circle of dough and let it prove or rise on a lightly oiled pizza tin. When the oven is hot spread a little of the olive oil over the surface of the dough and then put on both the cheeses, spreading them out equally all over the pizza but leaving a small border around the edge. Cut up the chilli and sprinkle the pieces over the cheese, add a pinch of salt and dribble on the rest of the olive oil. Take the pizza to the hot oven and bake it for about twenty minutes on a middle rack.

IL PROSCIUTTO, IL SALAME, LE SALSICCE
PARMA HAM, SALAMI, FRESH SAUSAGES

IL PROSCIUTTO   Parma Ham

A plateful of thin rosy slices of the best *prosciutto crudo*, especially when garnished by a slice of melon or a ripe dark fig has become a gastronomical cliché, but a cliché can be an endlessly repeated truth and the truth about *prosciutto crudo* is that it is a delicious and versatile food. *Prosciutto* is used in all manner of Italian dishes, in stuffings for *tortellini* and *cappelletti*, as wrappings for morsels of turkey or chicken, and as an added spice to vegetable dishes. It also make a popular and tasty addition to a pizza.

Prosciutto is sold in Italy in various kinds and qualities and it is very satisfying to stand in an old-fashioned food store and see the ranks of whole hams neatly hanging by their hooks in rows from the ceiling; under the glass-covered chilled counters there will be more hams already cut into, one of each variety. Some of the finest and most expensive hams come from the area around Parma where the pigs are fed on the whey left over from the making of parmesan cheese, which makes their flesh mild and delicate. The parma hams, too, are preserved with the minimum of salt and are hung to dry in currents of clear fresh air, which again enhances the sweetness of their flavour.

Very many people make the mistake of imagining that *prosciutto* is smoked as is French Bayonne ham, German Speck or the Italian *prosciutto di Sauris* from Friuli, but smoking gives an entirely different flavour, good, though less clear and direct. Smoked ham would entirely alter the character of dishes that use *prosciutto* as an additional flavouring such as *piselli al prosciutto* or *fave al prosciutto*, those delicious dishes of new peas and broad beans cooked with snippets of ham, sage, olive oil and stock. *Prosciutto* from San Danieli, a small town in the mountainous Friuli area of Italy, is a recognized and excellent quality ham a little redder in colour and slightly more salty than that from Parma. At San Danieli the pigs are allowed to roam and gorge themselves on acorns as in Roman and mediaeval days and so their flesh has a distinct and characteristic flavour.

All these finer hams are delicately trimmed and prepared, the cut side sealed with a suety fat which dries into a hard paste. Those from San Danieli come complete with the precisely pointed pig's trotter, a form

which is called *a coscia di capra*, goat's leg. The hams cured without the
trotter such as those from Parma are called *a coscia di pollo*, chicken's
leg or *a fiasco*, flask-shaped. The name of the provenance or manufacturer of the particular ham is seared crisply into the outer skin. There
are as yet only three types of *prosciutto* which have the *denominazione
di origine tutelata*, a state guarantee of quality and origin similar to that
awarded to good wines. These hams are those from Parma, San Danieli
and the Berico-Euganeo area of the Veneto, which produces a rose pink
ham even sweeter than that from Parma.

Occasionally (often, if you happen to be in that *salame* lover's para-
dise, Norcia, a small Umbrian town that specializes in pork products and
truffles) one can see wild boar hams, and in this case the brindled pelt is
left on the exterior side of the ham to differentiate the wild boars from
the pigs. Of course *prosciutto* is cured all over Italy and local varieties
are usually called *nostrano*, meaning 'ours' or home-cured. These hams
are generally robust, more salty in flavour and less delicate in texture
than Parma ham and in consequence cheaper in price. *Nostrano* hams
are usually cured without the trotter in the *a coscia di pollo* form and
their cut side is usually sealed with ground black peppercorns instead
of a fatty paste. While Parma hams are sometimes boned and so are able
to be cut with the finest precision on a mechanical slicer, the local hams
come complete and are sliced with a long flat sharp knife, and it requires some skill and experience to achieve fine, even and large slices.

All these recipes for pizza with *prosciutto* can also be made with *prosciutto cotto*, cooked ham. Unfortunately that most delicious dish of
one's childhood has now succumbed to the merciless advance of industrialized food; the blight of square, rubbery, wet ham is spreading. Even
in Italy the ugly pink blocks sully the counters of otherwise irreproach-
able food stores. However, in Italy there is less water injected into the
hams so when sliced very finely there still remains a hint of the soft
suede texture and delicate flavour of a home-cooked ham from a home-
killed pig. So when substituting cooked ham for Parma ham buy the best
quality that you can find; remember, the more water that the manufacturers can force into the hams the more profit they make and the less
meat, flavour and value you receive for your money.

Pizza al Prosciutto
Pizza with Parma Ham

prosciutto
mozzarella
green olives
olive oil

To make a Pizza al Prosciutto *you will need sufficient dough for a medium-size pizza base as given on page 29; 2 or 3 thin slices of* pros- ciutto *according to their size, preferably with a little fat attached to them; 6 oz/1 cup/170 g of mozzarella, thinly sliced; 7 or 8 pitted green olives; salt and freshly ground black pepper; 3 tablespoons of the best olive oil. Oven temperature: 425°F/220°C/7.*

Have your oven heating up to the requisite temperature. Roll out your circle of dough and place it in a lightly oiled flat tin. Leave the dough to rest while the oven heats.

Next brush a little of the olive oil over the pizza base. This lets the ham meld a little into the pizza dough rather than remain a dry layer. Lay the slices of *prosciutto* on top of the moistened dough, then cover them with the slices of mozzarella; the oil and the cheese will keep the ham from drying out, which it has a tendency to do in the heat of the oven. Scatter on the green olives, a slight sprinkle of salt and black pepper and last of all dribble on the remaining olive oil.

Place the pizza in the hot oven and let it cook for about twenty minutes or until the crust is golden and the cheese bubbles.

Pizza con Prosciutto e Polpa d'Oliva
Pizza with Parma Ham and Crushed Olives

mozzarella
prosciutto
olive pulp
olive oil

To make this savoury and unusual pizza you will need sufficient dough for one medium-size pizza base as given in the recipe on page 29; 6 oz/1 cup/170 g of mozzarella cut into small dice; 2 thin slices of prosciutto; *2 heaped tablespoons of olive pulp (see page 35); salt and plenty of freshly milled black pepper; 2 tablespoons of the best extra vergine olive oil. Oven temperature: 425°F/220°C/7.*

Take a large bowl and into it put the diced mozzarella and the ham cut into small irregular pieces; then add the olive pulp, if this is on the dry side moisten it with a little extra olive oil. Mix all the ingredients together with a fork until the cheese is coated with the olive pulp. Season it liberally with black pepper but use a light hand with the salt, as the *prosciutto* will provide its own supply.

Have the oven heating up while you roll out the dough into a disc and put it to prove on an oiled tin or floured board. All that remains to do is to spread the savoury mixture evenly over the pizza base, dribble on the olive oil, which must be of the best quality to compliment the crushed olives, and place the pizza in the hot oven to bake for twenty minutes. It will be cooked when the crust is a golden brown and the cheese melted and marbled with the porphyry-coloured olives.

Pomodori e basilica on a plate from Camucia

Wine jug from Gubbio with yellow peppers

Pizza al Prosciutto e Funghetti
Pizza with Parma Ham and Button Mushrooms

To make this delicious and popular pizza you will need, besides suffi-cient dough for a medium-size pizza base as given on page 29; 2 or 3 thin slices of prosciutto *according to their size; 4 oz/³⁄₄ cup/100 g of mozzarella cut into fine slices; 3 oz/¹⁄₂ cup/80 g of small tight button mushrooms shaved into fine slices; salt and freshly milled black pep-per; 3 tablespoons of* extra vergine *olive oil. Oven temperature: 425°F/220°C/7.*

> prosciutto
> mozzarella
> button
>   mushrooms
> olive oil

Have your oven heating up to the requisite temperature. Roll out your circle of dough and place it on a lightly oiled pizza tin. Leave the dough to rest while the oven heats.

Arrange the slices of ham and cheese on the dough, letting them overlap each other slightly. Next sprinkle on the delicately sliced mushrooms, letting most of them settle in a drift on òne side of the pizza, as they arrange them in my local pizzeria. Add a little salt and a few grinds of the black pepper mill. Finally dribble on the olive oil, making sure that most goes over the mushroom and ham to prevent them from wrinkling and drying in the heat.

Place the pizza in the fully heated oven and let it cook until the crust is golden and the cheese melted, about twenty minutes.

Pizza con Prosciutto e Pomodoro
Pizza with Parma Ham and Tomato

To make this pizza you will need sufficient dough for one medium-sized pizza base as given in the recipe oǹ page 29; 4 oz/¹⁄₂ cup/100 g of tomato pulp (see page 52); 2 or 3 thin slices of prosciutto, *cut into rib-bons about 1 inch wide; 4 oz/³⁄₄ cup/100 g of mozzarella cut into small dice; a sprinkle of salt, and instead of black pepper a little cayenne or chopped chilli pepper; 2 tablespoons of good olive oil. Oven temper-ature: 425°F/220°C/7.*

> tomato pulp
> prosciutto
> mozzarella
> cayenne
> olive oil

Whilst the oven is heating, roll out the dough and let it prove or rise on an oiled tin or floured board. Next spread on the tomato pulp, arrange the strips of *prosciutto* evenly and scatter on the mozzarella; sprinkle on a very little salt and a dusting of cayenne, as much as you enjoy, then add a generous dribble of olive oil. Put the pizza in the hot oven and bake it for twenty minutes.

IL SALAMI   Cured Sausage

There are numerous types of *salami* made in Italy. They usually contain pork or a mixture of pork and *vitello*, ox, and are seasoned with black pepper, sometimes garlic or white wine. The ground meat is packed into pig or ox intestines and these delicious *salami* are best when they are hard and mature. Each region of Italy boasts its own variation on the theme.

To my taste the best *salame* to use on a pizza is *salame di Napoli*. It is made up of lean pork, lean *vitello* and hard pork fat, and is seasoned with black pepper, salt, and *peperoncini*, hot dried chilli peppers. Sometimes garlic marinated in white wine is also used to add extra flavour. Usually the ground meat is stuffed into horse intestines, and the sausages are twelve to fourteen inches long. These *salami* are very often smoked over fires of green poplar wood, which gives a very particular flavour.

Pizza con Salame Piccante e Provolone
Pizza with Hot Spiced Salami and Provolone

tomato pulp
provolone
hot salame
olive oil

To dress a medium-size round pizza you will need sufficient dough from the recipe on page 29; 8 oz/1 cup/240 g of tomato pulp (see page 52); 3 oz/½ cup/80 g of provolone cheese, the mild kind, cut into dice; about 10 thin slices from a thin salame di Napoli *or a chilli-flavoured cured sausage; salt and black pepper; 2 tablespoons of olive oil. Oven temperature: 425°F/220°C/7.*

Have your oven heating up while you roll out the disc of dough and leave it to prove or rise on an oiled pizza tin. Next spread the tomato mixture over the dough, sprinkle on the diced cheese and arrange the slices of hot *salame* here and there over the pizza; add a little salt and pepper and, finally, dribble on the olive oil.

Place the pizza on the middle shelf of the oven and allow it to bake until the crust is golden, about twenty minutes. If the *salame* begins to curl, lower the heat after the initial ten minutes of baking.

LE SALSICCE   Fresh Sausages

Each small *macelleria*, that is butcher shop, in Italy makes their own sausages. There are, as far as I know, no large commercial firms that distribute fresh sausages around the country, although there are some famous companies that make and distribute *salame*. So, each butcher grinds up his own mixture of lean pork, salt and black pepper and stuffs it into washed ox intestines, dividing each sausage from its neighbour by loops of thin twine. Sometimes the sausages are made with the addition of pig's liver, which makes them very rich and savoury and they are then called *mazzafegati*. Other butchers add spices such as powdered *peperoncino*, dried chilli peppers, to very lean pork sausages and this imparts a gentle glow to the flavour. The main characteristics of these excellent Italian sausages are that they are usually fairly coarsely ground and contain good quality meat without gristle; apart from salt and pepper, garlic juice and occasionally spices there are no chemical additives, preservatives or any sort of cereal extenders. Displayed by the tray of sausages there will usually be a small handwritten notice describing their contents. Italian housewives buy two or three sausages at a time to crumble up and make into *ragu'*, a rich meat-laden pasta sauce. They also buy larger quantities to serve grilled as a main course, sometimes accompanied by slices of grilled polenta.

Italian sausages also make a very good addition to a pizza.

Pizza con Le Salsicce
Pizza with Fresh Pork Sausages

This pizza will have a splendid savoury taste if the sausage that you have selected is of a good and pure quality. Try and buy the sausages from an Italian delicatessen or, like the Italian butchers, coarsely grind up some pork with a little fat on it, adding to it salt, black pepper and the juice of two or three cloves of garlic crushed in muslin. Ordinary finely ground commercial sausages are not suitable substitutions.

tomato pulp
mozzarella
fresh pork
    sausages
parmesan
olive oil

To make a Pizza con Le Salsicce *you will need sufficient dough for a medium-size pizza base made according to the instructions on page 29; 8 oz/1 cup/240 g of tomato pulp (see page 52); 4 oz/³/₄ cup/100 g of mozzarella cut into thin slices; 2 or 3 Italian sausages according to their size; salt and freshly ground black pepper; 2 tablespoons of freshly grated parmesan; 2 tablespoons of green olive oil. Oven temperature: 425°F/220°C/7.*

Heat the oven while you roll out the circle of dough and leave it to prove or rise on an oiled tin or floured board. When the oven is hot start to dress the pizza.

First spread the tomato pulp over the dough, then place the mozzarella on top. Slit the skins of the sausages, remove the sausage meat and crumble it with your fingers, then scatter the pieces on top of the cheese; sprinkle on a little salt, a generous amount of black pepper and the grated parmesan. Finally trickle the olive oil over the surface of the pizza.

Place it in the hot oven where it will take about twenty minutes for the crust to become golden and the cheese to bubble. However, keep an eye on the sausage and if it seems to be in danger of burning reduce the heat a little.

Pizza con Salsicce e Funghi
Pizza with Sausages and Mushrooms

tomato pulp
button
  mushrooms
fresh pork
  sausages
parmesan or
  pecorino
olive oil

To make this pizza you will need sufficient dough for one medium-size pizza base made according to the recipe on page 29; 8 oz/1 cup/ 240 g of tomato pulp (see page 52); 2 oz/³⁄₄ cup/50 g of finely sliced button mushrooms; 2 Italian fresh pork sausages (see page 67 for information); 2 tablespoons of freshly grated parmesan or pecorino; salt and black pepper; 2 tablespoons of olive oil. Oven temperature: 425°F/220°C/7.

While the oven is heating, shape the pizza base and let it prove on an oiled pizza tin or floured peel.

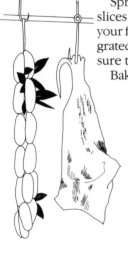

Spread the tomato over the proved dough and scatter on the fine slices of mushroom. Split the sausage skins, crumble the meat with your fingers and place it here and there over the pizza; sprinkle on the grated cheese, a little salt and black pepper, then the olive oil, making sure that the mushrooms have their share.

Bake the pizza for twenty minutes until the crust is golden.

LE CIPOLLE
ONIONS

All along the Ligurian coast of Italy stretching up and around to the French border then continuing along the southern coast of France, the local pizza is flavoured with onions. The name of the pizza changes at different points. In Italy it is known as *sardenaira* or *pizzalandrea* after the Italian Admiral Andrea Doria; further towards the French border it is called *pizza di ventimiglia* or *pisciadela*; in France itself, *pissaladière*. Until 1860 the coastal area up to and including Nice formed part of Italy and there are some Niçoise dishes that are closely tied to Italian, particularly Tuscan, recipes, both in name and ingredient.

The main difference between the French and Italian versions of this sunny Mediterranean dish is that while *pissaladière* contains onions, herbs, black olives, and anchovies or *pissala*, the Italian versions add tomato to this list. The name *pissaladière* comes not from pizza but from *pissala*, which is a strong-tasting paste made of tiny anchovies and sardines called in Nice *palaïa*. The larval anchovies, *poutine* in Nice, are the *cecinielli* much used in the *pizze* of 19th-century Naples. The layer of onions in the *pissaladière* was anointed with a cloth dipped into the fishy paste.

These coastal onion *pizze* are usually made with a base of bread dough enriched with olive oil and they are cooked in large oblong trays as opposed to the Neapolitan pizza baked on the floors of brick ovens. It has, in fact, become much more difficult to find a genuine *sardenaira* or *pissaladière*; modern examples sold in markets and bakeries tend towards a tomato-smeared pizza bread decorated with a little onion. While searching for *sardenaira* in Varazze, a small town in the middle of the Ponentine part of the Ligurian coast, an area where the *sardenaira* is supposed to be ubiquitous, time after time I was told that it did not exist. All the many *pizzerie* in the town claimed to be genuinely *Napoletana*. Perhaps southern *pizze* have overtaken and smothered the old local dish, whilst other old local dishes like *farinata*, a chickpea flour cake (see page 139), have flourished because there is nothing else like them.

Sardenaira
Ligurian Onion and Tomato Pizza

onions
tomatoes
black olives
anchovies
tomato
    concentrate
thyme
bay
olive oil

To make this pizza you will need all the dough produced with the recipe on page 29, to line an oblong pizza tray. Then, 2 lb/1 kg onions; 4 tablespoons of extra vergine olive oil or 3 tablespoons of saltless butter; salt and freshly milled black pepper; a large sprig of dried thyme and half a bay leaf; 2 lb/1 kg of fleshy, ripe Marmande tomatoes, skinned, seeded and chopped; 10 small dried black olives; 5 anchovy fillets; 5 more tablespoons of olive oil. Oven temperature: 425°F/220°C/7.

Peel the onions and slice them into very thin rounds with a sharp knife. Take a large flat sauté pan equipped with a lid and in it warm the 4 tablespoons of olive oil or the butter. Next add the onions and let them soften over a very low heat; season them with salt and pepper, the thyme and the bay leaf.

Cover the pan and let the onions become transparent in their own juice, they must not brown. After about forty-five minutes add the tomato pulp and tomato concentrate. Adjust the seasoning. Continue to simmer the mixture until the tomatoes are cooked, about fifteen minutes. If at this point there is a great deal of liquid in the pan, remove the lid, raise the heat and allow the mixture to reduce. Remove the pan from the heat and allow the contents to cool.

Meanwhile have the oven heating up while you roll out the dough to fit the tray. Oil the tray with some of the olive oil and line it with the dough, carrying it up the sides to make a small border. Pierce the surface of the dough here and there with the tines of a fork and let it prove for twenty minutes.

When the onions and tomato are cool spread them over the pizza base which you have moistened with a little oil. Add a little black pepper, arrange the olives and the anchovies and pour on the rest of the olive oil. Consign the pizza to the hot oven and bake it for twenty-five to thirty minutes.

Some people make *sardenaira* with raw onion. In this case the onions are peeled and sliced into thin rounds and laid on the dough base. The tomato, cooked in olive oil, is laid on top and then decorated with the olives and anchovies.

Pissaladière
Onion and Anchovy Pizza

The simple taste of this onion pizza depends on the quality and type of onion that you use. Indeed the degree of sweetness of an onion makes an immense difference to the flavour of any dish; for example a pasta sauce started off with a basic *trittata* of onion, carrot and celery will have a mellow soft taste if the onions and carrots are sweet and tender, a sweetness which will be picked up and enhanced by the ripe tomatoes added to them. If, however, the onions are acrid the sauce will be thin and bitter.

onions
black olives
anchovies
thyme
olive oil

For this recipe you will need sufficient dough to line a twelve inch round shallow tin, about half the quantity produced on page 29; 2 very large sweet onions (Valencia onions work well); 7 tablespoons of French extra vergine olive oil or 2 tablespoons of saltless butter; salt and freshly milled black pepper; a large sprig of dried thyme, dried at home if possible from fresh garden thyme; 6 small black olives, 4 or 5 anchovy fillets. Oven temperature: 425°F/220°C/7.

Peel the onions and slice them into very thin rounds with a sharp knife. Take a large flat sauté pan equipped with a lid and in it warm three tablespoons of the olive oil or the butter. Next add the onions and let them soften over a very low heat; season them with salt, pepper and the sprig of thyme. Cover the pan and let the onions become transparent in their own juice; they must not brown as this would alter the flavour, neither must they disintegrate into a mush.

Meanwhile have the oven heating up while you roll out the dough to fit the pizza tin. Oil the tin lightly with some of the olive oil and line it with the dough, carrying it up the shallow sides of the tin. Pinch the edge of the dough into a decoration if you wish and then pierce the surface here and there over the base with the tines of a fork. The dough should be a little less than a quarter of an inch thick. Leave the lined tin aside to prove for fifteen or twenty minutes.

When the onions are done to your satisfaction, which could take more than half an hour, spread them over the pizza base, which you have moistened with a little olive oil. Add a little more black pepper, arrange the olives and the anchovies broken into pieces, and pour on the rest of the olive oil in a thin stream over the surface. Consign the pizza to the hot oven where it will take about twenty minutes to bake. This *pissaladière*, cut into segments, will be sufficient for three or four people.

Pizza con Cipolle ed Uova Soda
Pizza with Onion and Egg

onions
eggs
parsley
olive oil

To make this pizza you will need sufficient dough for a medium-size base as given on page 29; 3 medium-sized sweet onions; 2 tablespoons of olive oil; possibly a spoonful or two of water; salt and black pepper; 2 eggs; a tablespoon of finely chopped parsley, the flat-leaved Mediterranean variety if possible. Oven temperature: 425°F/220°C/7.

Peel and slice the onions into fine circles. In a small sauté pan heat the olive oil over a gentle heat, add the onion and allow it to cook very gently until it has softened and is a pale blonde colour. Do not fry or burn it. If the onion becomes dry add a very little warm water. Season well with salt and freshly ground black pepper.

Meanwhile have your oven heating up. Roll out the disc of dough and lay it in the lightly oiled pizza tin. Let it rest and rise a little while the oven heats.

When the oven is hot and the onion cooked spread the mixture over the pizza base, consign it to the oven and let it cook until the crust is golden, about fifteen to twenty minutes. If the onion begins to look dry sprinkle on a little more olive oil.

While the pizza is cooking, put the fresh eggs into boiling water, let them cook for nine minutes, then plunge them immediately into cold water, shell them and slice into rounds. When the pizza is cooked arrange the sliced eggs over the surface, sprinkle on the chopped parsley and take immediately to the table.

I PEPERONI
BELL PEPPERS

In August my nearby Umbrian greengroceries are decorated with jewelly displays of scarlet, green, and marigold-yellow bell peppers. They are grown in the rich flat fields of the fertile valley of the Upper Tiber. The plants are extremely pretty; neat low bushes with dark glossy leaves. The flesh of the peppers is crisp and bursting with moisture. Local women, their heads shaded against the midday sun with wide-brimmed straw hats, gather the glowing crop and pack them into bright blue plastic crates.

Capsicums are actually native to the Americas and did not arrive in Europe until after Columbus. Like the tomato, they were a latecomer to the Italian kitchen. Perhaps the first comment on them was by Vincenzo Tanara, a *Bolognese* writer/cook. In his *L'Economia del Cittadino in Villa* of 1644, he mentions small American peppers which were dried then ground up and used instead of *zenzero*, ginger. Now, in Tuscany, a ground *peperoncino* (a small hot red pepper) is always called *zenzero*. I have never been able to elicit from any Tuscan the reason for this misnomer. Perhaps it dates from Tanara's 17th-century culinary substitution of the probably cheaper peppers for the more expensive ginger.

Peppers appear not to have played a great part in the cooking of the peninsula until Vincenzo Corrado, the Neapolitan cook/writer who dealt so beautifully with the tomato (see page 50), decided that they were worthy of consideration. In the 1781 edition of *Il Cuoco Galante* he gave a recipe for *I Peparoli Ripieni*, stuffed peppers. It is a dish still very popular in Naples today, with the Partenopean filling consisting of breadcrumbs, garlic, abundant parsley, black olives and capers. Another delicious component, which was also a novelty in Corrado's day, is the aubergine (eggplant).

Pizza is an excellent base for showing off the varied and succulent dishes that can be made with ripe shiny peppers. *Peperonata*, a soft stew of peppers, tomatoes and onions is very good when used on pizza with a little sharp cheese and a few capers. Brilliant red and orange *peperoni*, charred and peeled of their blackened skin and served with copious green olive oil and a salty anchovy or two, will also grace a pizza, enriched with a few black olives. There is also a delicious pasta sauce made of stewed red and yellow peppers, which are then put in a blender until they become a soft creamy orange mass; this mixed with diced mozzarella and garnished with a few fresh herbs like parsley and basil would make excellent and delicate *pizzette* for a first course.

Peperoni sott'Olio
Preserved Peppers

red or yellow peppers
garlic
olive oil

This delicious preserve is a fine accompaniment to cold meat and baked ham, is good puréed into a sauce for pasta, and excellent on top of a pizza as shown in the recipe on page 76.

To make this preserve you will need 6 ripe red or yellow peppers; 2 cloves of garlic; a little salt; olive oil as needed.

Choose really ripe taut glossy peppers. Cut them in half lengthways and remove the stems, seeds and membranes. Spear the pepper shells one at a time on a long-handled fork and hold it over a high gas flame, or place under an extremely hot electric grill or broiler. The skin of the pepper will bubble and blacken. If you do this slowly the flesh of the pepper will cook through gently. As each pepper-half blackens, put it into a covered saucepan to cool and steam in its own heat. When all the peppers are charred scrape off the black skin with a blunt knife, rinsing the peppers occasionally in cold water.

Slice the peppers into small strips and pack them tightly into perfectly clean and dry jars, adding a few slices of garlic and a very slight sprinkle of salt with each layer. Pour on the olive oil and, to make sure that there are no air pockets, do not seal the jars for several hours. As the peppers settle in the oil, air will rise to the surface. Leave a half inch strata of oil covering the peppers. The preserve will keep well when opened as long as there is a layer of oil above the peppers.

Peperonata
Stewed Bell Peppers

red and yellow peppers
tomatoes
onions
olive oil
wine·vinegar

This luscious *Peperonata* is wonderful hot with grilled meats or cold as an antipasto, and is splendid on a pizza garnished with chopped Mediterranean parsley and a few black olives. About 8 oz/1 cup/240 g is sufficient for a medium-size pizza.

To make a Peperonata *you will need 4 large peppers, 2 red and 2 yellow; 5 large ripe juicy tomatoes; 2 large sweet onions; 4 tablespoons of good olive oil; salt and black pepper; 1 tablespoon of wine vinegar.*

Split the peppers into halves lengthways, remove the stems, seeds and membranes, and cut the flesh into squares or fat strips. Deprive the tomatoes of their skins by dipping them into boiling water until they split, at which point the skins will be easy to slide away, and cut the flesh up into small segments. Peel the onions and chop them roughly.

In a large thick saucepan equipped with a lid, warm the olive oil; add all the vegetables, stir them around in the oil then put on the lid and let them cook gently over a low heat, checking occasionally to see that nothing is sticking or turning brown. Let them cook, *pianissimo*, in this way for about an hour. When the glowing orange stew is soft, season it with the salt and pepper, add the vinegar and let it cook uncovered a few more minutes until nearly all the liquid has evaporated.

Pizza con Peperoni ed Origano
Pizza with Bell Peppers and Oregano

This pizza has the sweet flavour of the south, the signature of the Mediterranean; it uses the tender flesh of yellow pepper, the strong scent of oregano, an undertone of garlic and of course the indispensable perfume of green olive oil. The most pungent and long-lasting variety of oregano, *rigani*, grows wild in Greece. I still have a little left of a bunch which I picked some years ago around the monastery built by St. Nectarius on Aegina and like a genie in a bottle the sweet scent still springs out when the jar is opened. Have by your side a few sprigs of sweet marjoram to strew on top of the pizza when you take it to the table. The fresh taste of this cousin of the dried oregano will add a subtle spice, a green note, to the flavour.

yellow pepper
onion
garlic
black olives
oregano
marjoram
olive oil

To make a medium-size pizza you will need sufficient dough made from the recipe on page 29. Then for the seasoning you will need 3 tablespoons of extra vergine olive oil; 2 fat fresh cloves of garlic; a sprinkle of freshly milled black pepper; 1 small onion, preferably the silvery fine-skinned variety, which you must chop; 1 yellow pepper cut into strips; a good pinch of oregano; 5 or 6 black olives; a few sprigs of fresh marjoram. Oven temperature: 425°F/220°C/7.

To cook the filling, gently heat up two tablespoons of the olive oil in a sauté pan, then add the garlic shaved into thin slices and a sprinkle of black pepper; allow these two ingredients to perfume the oil, the pepper will smell delicious. Add the chopped onion and allow it to hiss gently in the oil for a minute or so. Remember to keep the heat fairly low as the onion and garlic must not become brown and bitter.

Finally, add the yellow pepper and a pinch of oregano. Stir the mixture together and let it simmer over a low heat for about fifteen minutes until the pepper is just becoming tender and the onion is not quite translucent. The flavour will be sweet and mellow.

Meanwhile have the oven heating up. Roll out the disc of dough and let it prove or rise on an oiled pizza tin. For this particular pizza I prefer to roll the crust out finely so that it becomes light and crisp.

Spread the topping on to the disc of dough, decorate it with the black olives and splash on the remaining oil, about one tablespoon. Bake the pizza for twenty minutes until the crust is golden.

Before taking the pizza to the table, scatter on the fresh marjoram leaves.

This particular filling is not heavy as there is no cheese in it, and the pizza is splendid when cut into wedges and served hot as part of an antipasto or with well-chilled *aperitivi*.

Pizza con I Peperoni Rossi
Pizza with Red Bell Peppers

preserved
peppers
mozzarella
black olives
olive oil

Sun-ripened red bell peppers have their own wonderfully sweet flavour which can be given a deeper smokier tone by roasting them over a naked flame. One of the most delicious Italian salads consists of just these red and yellow peppers, roasted, split lengthways into strips, softened in strong olive oil and served simply on a dish covered in the oil in which they were cooked.

To make a medium-size pizza with this sweet smoky taste you will need sufficient dough made according to the recipe on page 29; 6 oz/1 cup/170 g of mozzarella; 4½ oz/a generous ½ cup/120 g of preserved peppers (see page 74); 6 or 7 black olives; salt and freshly ground black pepper; 2 tablespoons of green olive oil. Oven temperature: 425°F/220°C/7.

Have your oven heating up while you roll out the dough into a circle and place it to prove on an oiled tin or floured board. Slice the mozzarella into thin slices and lay them on top of the proved pizza base, then arrange the strips of pepper. Add a little salt and abundant black pepper, scatter on the olives and sprinkle the whole with the olive oil. Bake the pizza on the central shelf of the oven for twenty minutes.

Pizza con Peperoni e Pomodoro
Pizza with Bell Peppers and Tomato

Green bell peppers are simply those which have been picked before they have had a chance to ripen to a glowing yellow or a fiery red, and as they are underripe they have a tarter, less mellow flavour. Cut into narrow ribbons they make a crisp addition to a simple pizza garnished with tomato and garlic.

tomato pulp
green pepper
garlic
olive oil

To make a Pizza con Peperoni e Pomodoro you will need sufficient dough for a medium-size pizza base made according to the recipe on page 29; 8 oz/1 cup/240 g of tomato pulp (see page 52); 1 small green bell pepper or half a large one, cut into thin ribbons; 2 large cloves of garlic shaved into thin slices; 2 tablespoons of good flavourful olive oil; salt and black pepper. Oven temperature: 425°F/220°C/7.

While your oven is heating up, roll out the circle of dough and let it prove or rise on an oiled tin. Next, spread the tomato pulp on the pizza, arrange the pepper strips and scatter on the sliced garlic. Dribble on the olive oil evenly, and add a sprinkle of salt and a good few turns of the pepper mill. Place the pizza in the hot oven and let it bake for about twenty minutes or until the crust is golden.

I CARCIOFI
ARTICHOKES

The elegant artichoke, *al harsuf* in Arabic, was brought to Sicily in the 1400s, probably by way of the silk trade between the Italians and the Nasrids, the last blossoms of Spanish Islam.

The delicate vegetable became the darling of Renaissance *buongustai*, lovers of good food, both for its flavour and its decorative appearance. Indeed Catherine di Medici took her predilection for them to excess and nearly died of over-indulgence at a wedding party in 1575. Caravaggio, infamous for his uncertain temper, threw a tray of artichokes at a tavern waiter in 1604 when the latter suggested that the painter stick his nose into them and discover for himself which were cooked in butter and which in oil.

Cristofaro di Messisbugo, one of Italy's greatest cooks, gives a recipe in his 'New Book' published in 1557 for a *pastello di carchioffoli* which is an ancestor of the modern Italian *torta di carciofi*. Artichokes were enjoyed, too, simply served in a little beef stock in which they had been cooked then seasoned with parmesan and pepper, a pleasant idea, easy to revive. Cooks made pies of artichokes, oysters and beef marrow. They were boiled and served cold in salads, sliced and fried as they are today, and even wrapped in caul like pieces of liver and grilled on a spit over a wood fire. There is a magnificent fast day recipe dating from 1664 for artichokes stuffed with fish, oysters, prawn tails and truffles.

My friend Silvana Cerotti always has a few artichokes growing in her kitchen garden although she does not cut them for eating. Instead she lets them flower until the magnificent purple blooms are withered and brown. When the moon is in a propitious phase she gathers the heads and separates the dried stamens. These she uses to make a vegetable rennet to separate her pecorino cheese.

Today, Italians, unlike us, are not prone to serving a boiled round artichoke to be eaten slowly in tiny mouthfuls liberally irrigated with melted butter or hollandaise until the secret delicious heart is freed; the reward for patience. In Italy the artichoke is cheap and plentiful, picked when young and tender and cooked and eaten with different ceremony.

During the spring and also in November you may see great piles of them outside vegetable shops and in the markets, sold complete with long stalks and shaggy leaves. Slim and spear-shaped, their dull green outer leaves streaked with purple, the small sweet artichokes seem to be the most popular variety although the fat round Roman sort, *mamme romane*, are best for stuffing.

Because the artichoke in Italy is so plentiful many people use the hearts alone and put them up in jars to be used as part of an *antipasti*, a course of interesting and appetite-provoking savouries that precedes the pasta course at luncheon. These preserved artichokes may also be used in the seasoning of a good pizza.

Carciofi sott'Olio alla Mariella
Artichokes Preserved in Olive Oil

artichokes
lemons
white wine
cloves
bay leaves
peppercorns
white wine
    vinegar
olive oil

Some of the most flavourful preserved artichoke hearts that I have eaten were prepared by my friend Mariella Morandi Gamurrini who lives in Arezzo, and I include her recipe which is a useful one for anyone lucky enough to have access to an abundant crop of tender young artichokes. Mariella says that the best artichokes to preserve are the small ones, the starvelings that are the last to be gathered from the plants. They are not in evidence every year, so, in consequence, are a welcome special event when they do appear in the market.

You will need 1 lb/450 g of small and tender artichokes picked before the choke has developed; the juice of 2 lemons; 36 fl oz/4 cups/1 litre of good white wine; 18 fl oz/2 cups/500 ml good white wine vinegar; the peel of 1 small lemon; 3 cloves; 2 bay leaves; 1½ teaspoons of salt and 6 black peppercorns. To put the finishing touches to the jars you will need an extra clove, bay leaf and 2 peppercorns for each jar, and olive oil as needed.

Clean and trim the artichokes of all the hard outer leaves until you are left with what you are sure are the tender inner ones; cut the points off these and trim the bases into neat round shapes. As you work put the artichokes into a bowl of cold water acidulated with the juice of 2 lemons.

In a stainless steel or enamel pan mix the wine and the vinegar, then add the lemon peel, cloves, bay leaves, salt and peppercorns. Bring the liquid to the boil, drop in the drained and dried artichokes and let them boil for ten minutes. Drain the artichokes thoroughly, let them cool and arrange them packed tightly together in perfectly clean and dry preserving jars. Add to each jar a fresh clove, bay leaf and two peppercorns.

Pour the olive oil over the artichokes until they are completely covered but do not seal the jars for a few hours, as pockets of air will come to the surface as the artichokes settle in the oil. Finally, cover the artichokes with at least half an inch of oil, close the lids tightly and store the preserve in a dark place where they will keep well. Once opened, make sure the artichokes remain under the layer of oil.

These make a delicious accompaniment to cold meats and chicken, are good as an antipasto with a soft white cheese such as a *tom* from Turin, or split and used to flavour a pizza.

Pizza con I Carciofi
Pizza with Artichokes

artichokes
mozzarella
olive oil

To make a medium-size pizza you will need sufficient dough from the recipe on page 29; 2 very small or 1 large young spear-shaped artichokes; juice of 1 lemon; 3 tablespoons of olive oil; salt and black pepper; 6 oz/1 cup/170 g of mozzarella; 2 more tablespoons of good olive oil. Oven temperature: 425°F/220°C/7.

First of all clean and trim the artichokes of their outer leaves; how many layers you will have to remove depends of course on the particular artichokes that you are dealing with, however this recipe is intended for ones that are so young that the choke has not yet developed. If you are using a large artichoke, strip off the tough leaves and cut the head in half to remove the choke. When each artichoke has been trimmed, cut it into thin slices from top to stem and throw each slice into acidulated water to prevent the flesh becoming black. Leave them in the water until you are ready to cook them.

Have your oven heating up while you roll out the dough into a circle and let it prove or rise on an oiled tin. Heat the three tablespoons of oil in a shallow pan then add the slices of artichoke which you have removed from their bath, rinsed and patted dry with a clean cloth. Let them soften gently in the oil and season them with salt and pepper.

Slice the mozzarella into thin rounds and arrange these upon the disc of dough; when the artichoke is almost tender spread the slices on top of the cheese, if necessary dribbling on the extra oil and more salt and pepper. Bake the pizza for twenty minutes until the crust is golden and the cheese is melted.

Wild mushrooms and vine leaves in Tuscany

Sweet scented basil and tomatoes in a yellow ware bowl

Pizza con Carciofi sott'Olio e Pomodoro
Pizza with Preserved Artichokes and Tomato

To make this medium-size pizza you will need sufficient dough made according to the recipe on page 29; 8 oz/1 cup/240 g of tomato pulp (see page 52); 2 oz/less than ½ cup/50 g of coarsely grated fontina; 5 preserved artichoke hearts (see page 79); 7 or 8 capers; salt and freshly ground black pepper; 2 tablespoons of olive oil. Oven temperature: 425°F/220°C/7.

tomato pulp
preserved
   artichokes
fontina
capers
olive oil

Have your oven heating up while you roll out the dough into a disc and let it prove or rise on an oiled tin or floured peel.

On the dough spread a layer of the tomato pulp. Sprinkle on the grated fontina, then arrange the artichoke hearts split into halves if they are tiny or thirds if they are large. Add the capers here and there, add salt and a generous spray of black pepper and finally dribble on the olive oil.

Bake the pizza for twenty minutes or until the crust is golden and the cheese bubbles.

LE MELANZANE
AUBERGINES (Eggplants)

The aubergine or eggplant is one of the most beautiful of vegetables, whether it is a satiny midnight purple or pale as delicately tinted ivory. And although the flavour remains the same, the colour, to some people, is of prime importance. In the *souk* at Luxor where I used to shop for our expedition supplies I once followed a woman right down the long length of the market street because I was puzzled by her behaviour. At each stall that sold aubergines (*beidindjaan*, 'Devil's eggs', in Arabic) she would stop and search diligently through the piles of dark or striped vegetables. It seemed that not one aubergine pleased her. Eventually she found some that met with her approval, although to me they appeared to be very much like all the others. Later I asked my cook Ahmed what he thought she had been doing. The aubergine, he said, can be fortunate or unfortunate all according to its markings and colour. The woman had been searching for a precise shade and shape to bring good fortune to her family. In Italy the aubergine was also, at one time, regarded with caution.

The aubergine or eggplant, probably native to India, was known in Italy in the 14th century and was widely cultivated in the 15th, but initially, as was the tomato, *melanzane* were regarded with great suspicion – the *mela-insana* was thought to trouble the minds of those who ate them, to send them mad. Perhaps this strange idea came from a mistaken interpretation of the Turkish dish *Imam Bayeldi*, the Imam Fainted, meant to imply that the worthy muselman lost conciousness from pleasure but taken by the Italians to mean that the dish was a danger to those of sound mind.

Cristofaro di Messisbugo in his elegant 16th-century cookery book gives a recipe for aubergines filled with cheese, eggs, spices and aromatic herbs, which were then tied up to prevent the stuffing from escaping and poached in broth. Stuffed aubergines or eggplants are still enjoyed in Italy today but are baked in the oven not cooked in *brodo*. Southern Italians are partial to their aubergines cooked *al parmigiano* – that is, done in the oven with a rich tomato sauce and a great deal of nutty parmesan in a medium of fruity olive oil. The soft earthy taste of the aubergine marries well with these flavours. They also like them split lengthways, scattered with chopped garlic and *peperoncino*, basted with olive oil and then baked in the oven. In Calabria they are often preserved under oil and eaten as a relish with cold meats; they are, in this form, very good on pizza.

The aubergine will look prettier on the pizza if it is the dark purple-black variety – the flavour will be the same as the pale ivory or white violet-streaked kinds, but the appearance of the skin should be the deciding factor.

Melanzane sott'Olio della Signora Cetraro
Signora Cetraro's Aubergines (Eggplants) Preserved under Oil

aubergines
  (eggplant)
white wine
olive oil
garlic
white wine
  vinegar
red chilli
  peppers
mint

This preserve can be used in a *Pizza Quattro Stagione* as a sharp element instead of the more usual preserved artichoke heart (see page 47 for the recipe). It will also make an interesting addition to the filling of a *calzone*, again taking the place of artichoke.

To make this delicious preserve you will need 2 large aubergines (eggplants), about 2 lb/1 kg; coarse salt as needed; 18 fl oz/2 cups/500 ml of white wine; 9 fl oz/1 cup/250 ml of white wine vinegar; 9 fl oz/1 cup/ 250 ml of olive oil; 2 large cloves of garlic; 2 sprigs of mint; 2 red chilli peppers; extra olive oil as needed.

Peel the aubergines and slice them lengthways then widthways into thin sticks. As you cut them, drop them into a china bowl and sprinkle them liberally with salt. Sprinkle salt on top of the bowl of aubergine and weight it down with a heavy object on top of a plate. Leave the aubergine to drain away its bitter juices for several hours or even over-night. The bulk of the aubergine will reduce by half after the water content is dispersed.

When you are ready to cook the aubergine squeeze the pieces to be rid of the juice and rinse them well to remove the salt. Taste a piece to be sure that the rinsing was adequate. Heat the wine and vinegar in a stainless steel or aluminium saucepan and boil the aubergine in this mixture for five minutes. At the end of this drain them well and pat dry.

In a large mixing bowl combine the olive oil, the garlic cut into sliv-ers, the mint chopped into coarse fragments and the two chillis chopped into small pieces. Add to this bowl of seasoning the auber-gine and stir all around until evenly mixed.

Have ready several clean and perfectly dry preserving jars; fill them with the spiced aubergine, pressing the preserve well into the jars. Pour more olive oil over the aubergine, making sure that the preserve is covered by at least half an inch of oil. Leave the jars unsealed for a while so that the preserve may settle in the oil, which can be topped up with more oil if needed.

Store the jars in a dark place, where they will keep well once opened, but make sure the aubergine is covered with a layer of olive oil.

Pizza al Melanzane
Pizza with Aubergines (Eggplant)

To make a Pizza al Melanzane *you will need sufficient dough from the recipe on page 29 to make a medium-size pizza base; 1 medium-size aubergine (eggplant); coarse salt; 4 tablespoons of olive oil; 2 crushed cloves of garlic; 8 oz/240 g of fresh tomatoes, skinned, seeded and chopped, or the same amount of tomato pulp prepared according to the recipe on page 52; 6 or 7 black olives; salt and freshly ground black pepper; 1 teaspoon of dried oregano (see note on page 37); 2 tables-poons of* extra vergine *olive oil if required. Oven temperature: 425°F/220°C/7.*

aubergine
  (eggplant)
tomato pulp
black olives
garlic
oregano
olive oil

First of all wash your aubergine and cut off the prickly green stem, then slice the aubergine into circles about the depth of the pink of

your little fingernail. Cut these circles into dice and put them into a colander, salting each handful lightly as you put them in. On top put a small plate or saucer and weight it down with some convenient heavy object (for years I have used the iron weight from an old steel yard which I bought in a village market when we first lived in Italy). Let the aubergine alone for about thirty minutes and during this time the brown bitter juice will ooze away; the aubergine will soften in texture and will not absorb quite so much olive oil when it is fried. After thirty minutes rinse the aubergine briefly under a running tap to be rid of the excess salt and dry well with a clean cloth or some paper towels.

Heat up the oil in a large sauté or frying pan and add the crushed cloves of garlic; when they are just about to turn colour add the diced aubergine and fry the pieces briskly until they too are about to turn golden. Remove from the heat and set aside.

Meanwhile, with your oven heating to the requisite temperature, roll out the disc of dough and place it on an oiled pizza tin, or floured peel if you are going to bake on tiles. Let the dough prove or rise until the oven is hot.

Spread the tomato pulp on to the dough, distribute the aubergine evenly on top, scatter the black olives in a rough pattern, then add a little salt, black pepper and a generous dusting of oregano. If the aubergines have soaked up all the oil, add a little more fresh olive oil if it seems necessary – the filling should not become dried out in the heat of the oven.

Bake the pizza in the oven – it will be cooked after about twenty minutes or when the edges of the crust are golden.

Pizza con Melanzane e Mozzarella
Pizza with Aubergines (Eggplant) and Mozzarella

aubergine
　(eggplant)
mozzarella
garlic
oregano
olive oil

For this recipe you will need 1 medium-size purple-black aubergine (eggplant); salt; 4 tablespoons of good olive oil; 2 crushed cloves of garlic. Then you will need sufficient dough for a medium-sized pizza base, made according to the recipe on page 29; 6 oz/1 cup/170 g of mozzarella cut into small dice; 1 teaspoon of dried oregano (see note on page 37); salt and a generous amount of black pepper; 2 tablespoons of excellent quality extra vergine *olive oil. Oven temperature: 425°F/220°C/7.*

Treat the aubergine in exactly the same way as it is prepared in the previous recipe, that is slice it into circles, dice, salt, leave to drain, then rinse and dry. Heat up the oil, add the crushed garlic and when it is just about to turn colour add the diced aubergine and fry lightly. Remove and set aside.

Do not neglect to have your oven heating up as pizza requires a lively hot oven for success. Roll out your circle of dough and leave it to prove or rise on an oiled tin or floured peel. Take a fairly commodious bowl and into it put the fried aubergine and diced mozzarella. Mix them together lightly with a fork then tip them on to the dough and spread them out evenly.

Sprinkle on the oregano, salt and several turns of the black pepper mill. (Alternatively crush some black peppercorns, about four or five, between paper and sprinkle on these coarse grains.) Finally dribble on the olive oil.

Consign the pizza to the hot oven where it will require about twenty minutes to cook the dough to a golden brown.

Pizza con Melanzane e Parmigiano
Pizza with Aubergines (Eggplant) and Parmesan

You will first need 1 medium-size aubergine (eggplant); salt; 4 tablespoons of good olive oil; 2 fat crushed cloves of garlic. Then you will need sufficient dough for a medium-size pizza base made according to the recipe on page 29; 4 oz/100 g of tomatoes, skinned, seeded and chopped; 3 or 4 sprigs of parsley, roughly chopped, salt and black pepper; 4 tablespoons of coarsely grated or crumbled parmesan; a little more olive oil to sprinkle on top of the pizza. Oven temperature: 425°F/220°C/7.

aubergine
 (eggplant)
tomatoes
garlic
parmesan
parsley
olive oil

Treat the aubergine as described in the recipe on page 83 – slice into circles, dice, salt, leave to drain and then rinse and dry.

Have the oven heating up while you roll out your disc of dough, and leave it to prove or rise while you cook the filling. To do this heat up the olive oil in a flat sauté pan or shallow saucepan, add the crushed garlic and cook it until it is at the point of turning gold; do not let it brown or burn. Then add the diced aubergine and cook rapidly over a lively heat tossing the pieces about in the hot oil. When they are beginning to change colour add the chopped tomato; stir the ingredients together, then add the chopped parsley, salt and plenty of black pepper. Leave the pan to simmer over a gentle heat until you are left with a fairly dry mixture.

Spread the mixture evenly on to the dough and sprinkle the grated parmesan on top. Place in the hot oven and cook for about twenty minutes; half-way through the cooking look and make sure that the parmesan is not drying out, if it is, sprinkle on a little more olive oil and continue with the baking.

I FUNGHI, I TARTUFI
MUSHROOMS, TRUFFLES

I FUNGHI   Mushrooms

The ancient Romans appreciated wild *funghi* and cautious senator gourmets would prepare stews of mushrooms with their own hands, being fearful of the inclusion of 'ambiguous toadstools' whether by accident or, in those turbulent days, design.

Today, in Italy, *funghi* gathering in the summer and early autumn is a national pastime, so much so that stringent conservation laws have had to be passed in certain regions to protect the *funghi*. The most sought-after are *amanita caesarea*, or *ovoli*, delicately flavoured, orange-yellow smooth-capped mushrooms; they are rare and expensive and very often served raw, shaved into thin slices mixed with similarly sliced truffles and seasoned simply with olive oil and lemon juice. Of course they are also used in exquisite pasta sauces and delicate soups.

Porcini, Lat. *boletus edulis*, Fr. *cèpes*, are another Italian favourite whether stewed with wild savory, fried, or grilled with olive oil and garlic. When there is a glut they are sliced and dried ready to be used in sauces during the cold months of the year. These dried *porcini*, now easily available in most good food stores, are excellent when added to dishes of ordinary cultivated mushrooms to enliven their flavour.

Chanterelles, It. *giallini*, Lat. *cantharellis cibarius*, are the exquisitely flavoured and apricot-scented yellow mushrooms that grow wild in the shelter of pine and chestnut forests. At the crossroads in Palazzo del Pero, a small Tuscan hamlet south of Arezzo, there are usually groups of men and women to be found sitting by the roadside in the summer sun; beside them are dainty baskets of wild *funghi* which they have risen early to collect. This area of Tuscany is famous for the quantity and quality of mushrooms that proliferate there. The chanterelles from Palazzo del Pero are especially luscious and one way to retain their fresh-scented flavour in a pizza is to protect them under mozzarella cheese.

During the last few years *funghi coltivati* – our button mushrooms – have become more popular in Italy and are now to be found in most *supermercati* and city greengrocers. Similarly it is usual to find a *Pizza ai Funghi* on the menu of most *pizzerie*.

Pizza alla Boscaiola
Pizza with Porcini

This type of pizza, using a local ingredient instead of an item native to Naples, has become very popular in Umbria in those places where *porcini* grow in great profusion. A few of the mushrooms, combined with a little tomato, some *prosciutto* and a spoonful or so of good parmesan, make an unusual pizza. In Italy *porcini* are stewed in a little olive oil before being put on to a pizza. Fresh *porcini* are not easily come by in other countries but dried ones are to be found in good food stores and they will suffice to add their particular flavour to this pizza.

dried porcini
tomato pulp
prosciutto
parmesan
parsley
olive oil

To make it you will need sufficient dough for a medium-size pizza base as given on page 29; 1 oz/1 cup/25 g of dried porcini; 8 oz/1 cup/ 240 g of tomato pulp (see page 52); 1 large slice of prosciutto; *2 tablespoons of fresh coarsely grated parmesan; 1 tablespoon of chopped parsley; 2 tablespoons of olive oil. Oven temperature: 425°F/220°C/7.*

Put the dried mushrooms in a bowl, pour over them a ladleful of boiling water, let them soak in this for half an hour, then squeeze them dry and chop them roughly with a sharp knife; the liquid, strained to remove any grit, can be used for soups or sauces.

With the oven heating up, roll out the circle of dough and let it prove or rise on an oiled pizza tin or floured peel. Spread the tomato pulp on the proved dough; on one side of the circle place the *prosciutto* torn into large fragments, on the other spread the mushrooms. Sprinkle the parmesan all over the pizza, then add the parsley and finally the olive oil, making sure that the *prosciutto* has a light covering as should the mushrooms.

Bake the pizza for twenty minutes until the crust is golden.

In Italy one can buy small graters especially designed to slice truffles, usually made of stainless steel and with one sharp fine blade which is regulated by a screw; they provide very fine slices. Many Italian restaurateurs use this slicer to shave parmesan too, and the texture of the flakes of cheese produced with one of these gadgets is perfect in a salad of *ovoli* and truffles and for the cheese on this pizza.

Pizza ai Funghi
Pizza with Button Mushrooms

mozzarella di
  bufala
button
  mushrooms
olive oil

Perhaps the best mushroom-filled pizza that I have ever tasted was the one served in the famous restaurant 'Gigino, Pizza al Metro' in Vico Equense, a short drive along the coast from Naples. The pizza came in a half-metre length and had the slightly sour taste of genuine mozzarella, which had fused perfectly into the crust, and flavourful *funghi* which were bathed in good oil.

To make this soft delicious pizza you will need sufficient dough for one medium-size pizza base made from the recipe on page 29; 3 tablespoons of good olive oil; 6 oz/1 cup/170 g of mozzarella, di bufala if obtainable; 4 oz/1¼ cups/100 g of finely sliced button mushrooms; salt and black pepper. Oven temperature: 425°F/220°C/7.

While the oven is heating up, roll out the dough into a circle and let it prove or rise on an oiled tin or floured peel. Paint one tablespoon of the olive oil over the risen dough then lay on top the mozzarella, cut into thin slices. Leave a small border around the edge so that the cheese does not escape over the edge of the pizza when it melts. Scatter the fine mushroom slices on top of the cheese, letting them overlap like tiles. Sprinkle on a little salt and a few grains of black pepper.

Lastly, gently dribble on the remaining two tablespoons of olive oil, making sure that the mushrooms have a light but adequate cover to protect them from drying out and wrinkling in the heat of the oven.

Bake the pizza for twenty minutes or until the crust is golden and the cheese bubbling.

Pizza con Funghi e Pomodori
Pizza with Mushrooms and Tomatoes

tomatoes
button
  mushrooms
basil
olive oil

Another delicious way to use mushrooms in a pizza is to combine them with fresh tomatoes and fresh basil leaves. For this pizza to be successful you need ripe but firm tomatoes that are flavourful and not the least bit watery. It will probably be more satisfactory to use one very large or two medium-size Marmande (beefsteak) tomatoes, which by their nature are fleshy and will give you more substance and flavour .

To make this pizza you will need sufficient dough for one medium-size pizza base made according to the instructions on page 29; 2 medium or 1 large Marmande tomatoes that you have peeled, seeded and chopped; 5 or 6 fresh basil leaves; 3 oz/³⁄₄ cup/80 g of finely sliced firm button mushrooms; 3 tablespoons of green olive oil; salt and black pepper. Oven temperature: 425°F/220°C/7.

Have your oven heating up while you roll out your circle and let it prove on an oiled pizza tin. Arrange the tomato pulp on the dough and place two or three of the basil leaves upon it. Then scatter on the finely sliced mushroom and sprinkle on the olive oil, watching to see that the mushrooms are lightly covered. Add a little salt and pepper.

Place the pizza in the hot oven and cook for about twenty minutes. Before you serve the pizza arrange upon it the remaining basil leaves.

When using dried herbs to season a pizza it is of course perfectly logical to add the seasoning before the pizza goes into the oven but in the case of fresh basil leaves it seems to me unnecessary to desiccate their succulent greenness, so some of the leaves are put under the mushrooms to flavour the tomato without becoming crisped up and the remainder are used as a fresh garnish.

Pizza con I Funghi Trifolati
Pizza with Truffled Mushrooms

Trifolati is a word used in Umbria to denote a way of preparing mushrooms; it has no connection with *trifoglio*, a trefoil, but is a corruption of *tartufati*, truffled. *Funghi trifolati* are usually served as a *contorno*, a vegetable dish to adorn the main course of the meal. They also make a splendid and rich seasoning on a pizza and are good too in an open *torta*, a tart made with fleur pastry (see page 155 for a recipe for this pastry).

button
 mushrooms
garlic
parsley
tomato
 concentrate
olive oil

To make sufficient funghi trifolati *to season one medium-size pizza or four* pizzette *(the dough made according to the instructions on page 29); you will need 9 oz/2½ cups/240 g of firm button mushrooms; 2 small cloves of garlic; 2 tablespoons of olive oil; 1 tablespoon of tomato concentrate; 2 heaped tablespoons of chopped parsley; salt and freshly ground black pepper; extra chopped parsley for garnish if desired. Oven temperature: 425°F/220°C/7.*

Clean and trim the button mushrooms and slice them finely and evenly. Clean the cloves of garlic and slice them finely too. Heat the olive oil in a shallow sauté or frying pan, put in the sliced garlic to soften, then add the mushrooms and turn them well in the oil; lower the heat and allow the mushrooms to give up their liquid. At this point add the tomato concentrate and mix it well with the *funghi* juice.

Sprinkle on the parsley and season with a little salt and black pepper

– be careful with the pepper as mushrooms assume flavours very easily. Cook the mushrooms for about ten minutes on a fairly low heat so that the juices evaporate, but beware that they do not dry out too much.

Have your oven heating up while you roll out the dough into a medium-size pizza or, alternatively, into four small *pizzette*. Let them prove or rise on an oiled pizza tin or a floured board. Divide the cooked mushrooms evenly between the small *pizze* or spread them over the large pizza according to your choice.

Sprinkle on a little olive oil and put in the oven to bake, twenty minutes for the pizza and ten to fifteen minutes for the *pizzette*. They will be cooked when the crusts are a pretty golden colour. If you wish, sprinkle on a little more chopped parsley, and serve immediately.

Pizza con I Giallini
Pizza with Chanterelles

chanterelles
mozzarella
parsley
butter
olive oil

This pizza makes a most elegant first course for a dinner party served with a delicate white wine. The flavours of the *funghi* and the cheese marry well together. You could slice one medium-size pizza for four first course servings, or you could serve this filling on tiny individual *pizzette*.

You will need sufficient dough for a medium-size pizza base made according to the recipe on page 29; 8 oz/2½ cups/240 g of chanterelles; 2 walnut-size pieces of saltless butter; salt and white pepper; 6 oz/1 cup/170 g of mozzarella sliced into thin rounds; a little good Ligurian olive oil; 1 tablespoon of finely chopped parsley. Oven temperature: 425°F/220°C/7.

First clean the chanterelles with a damp cloth and split the large ones by tearing them along the grain from stem to top. Melt the butter in a flat pan, add the *funghi* and let them cook gently until their juices run, taking great care that they do not brown. Allow them to simmer for a few minutes until the small sauce formed in the pan by the butter and mushroom liquid has reduced a little, then season them with a little salt and a little white pepper.

Meanwhile, as the oven is heating up, roll out the circle of dough and let it prove or rise on an oiled pizza tin or floured board. Arrange a few of the slices of mozzarella on the proved dough, add the *funghi*, cover them with more of the mozzarella to keep them juicy in the heat of the oven, sprinkle on the olive oil and bake the pizza for twenty minutes until the crust is golden. Sprinkle on the chopped parsley and take the pizza to the table immediately.

I TARTUFI Truffles

There is a very luxurious version of a mushroom pizza which is not to be found on the menu of ordinary *pizzerie*. It includes the magical white truffle that has made Alba famous all over the world. There is no adequate way to describe the taste of a fresh white truffle to anyone who has not eaten one, except to say that they have not so much a taste as a scent. Taste and smell are so closely allied anyway as to be but aspects of the same faculty, but the scent of the truffle has the ability to enhance the taste of anything that it accompanies. To make the most of this mysterious quality it is best to use the truffle in the simplest of ways, and to eat it raw or at most warmed to a slight degree.

In certain areas of Umbria, particularly around the upper reaches of the Tiber Valley, the truffle, both black and white, is to be found in surprising quantity and quality. In the small Umbrian town in which I do much of my food shopping the grocery shops occupy the ground floor stone-vaulted rooms of mediaeval *palazzi*. One winter day, stepping into the dim-lit depths of one of these shops, I was immediately surrounded by the heady, overpowering scent of white truffles. At the counter stood a *contadino* dressed in extremely old and worn velvet breeches and tattered jacket. Today, still, in modern Italy there are some people living in the depths of rural areas who look almost sylvan in their appearance. They rarely venture into the towns, perhaps once or twice a year for the large fairs or when they have something to sell. Their hands are cracked and ingrained with soil, their hair is long and their faces are wrinkled and deep brown from the sun and wind. They have a scent of foxes and forests about them. The country man had brought out of his pocket a brown paper package which he unfolded and handed to the grocer. In the paper were five large sand-coloured truffles. The grocer prised off a few pieces of earth that encrusted the tubers and examined them closely to estimate their size, as one of the tricks of the truffle trade is to leave pieces of mud, which weigh heavy, clinging to the crevices of the truffle. The grocer smelt them, weighed them and paid the man who left, pleased. The truffles were put into a large wickerwork basket nearly full of the intoxicatingly strong-scented tubers. These were destined for famous Milanese restaurants and were worth a considerable sum of money. However, both the *contadino* and the rich clients of the great restaurants eat the truffles with pleasure, the latter knowing and appreciating that the exquisitely cooked dish served to him is closely tied in substance and inspiration to the land.

Pizza al Tartufo Bianco
Pizza with White Truffles

parmesan
mozzarella di
bufala
white truffle
olive oil

To make this pizza you will need sufficient dough for one medium-size pizza as given in the recipe on page 29; 4 oz/1 cup/100 g of freshly grated parmesan; 6 oz/1 cup/170 g of genuine mozzarella di bufala, diced; 2 tablespoons of the best Ligurian extra vergine olive oil; salt and a little freshly ground white pepper; a white truffle the size of a walnut. Oven temperature: 425°F/220°C/7.

Have your oven heating up while you roll out your circle of dough and leave it to prove or rise on a flat oiled tin or a floured board.

In a bowl mix together lightly the grated parmesan and the diced mozzarella, tip it out on to the dough and spread it over the surface, leaving a small border so that the melting cheese does not escape over the edge. Dribble on the olive oil and scatter a little salt and white pepper.

As soon as the oven is at the correct temperature put in the pizza and let it bake for about twenty minutes or until the crust is golden and the cheese melted. Immediately you take the pizza from the oven grate the truffle over it so that the fine ivory marbled slices fall and stick on the soft hot cheese. If you do not have a truffle grater, before the pizza is quite done cut the truffle into the thinnest slices that you can manage with the aid of a very sharp knife and scatter these on to the pizza.

Serve the pizza or, indeed, the *pizzette*, as a first course with a good dry sparkling Italian white wine or a champagne.

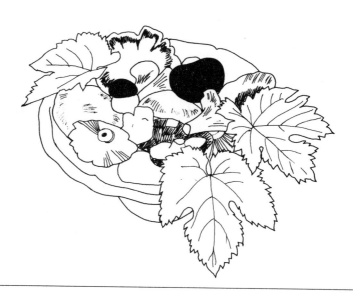

I PESCI
FISH

Pliny the Younger wrote that he could stand at a window of his villa on Lake Como and cast a line directly into the lake to catch a fish for his supper. Around the shores of the peninsula both Greeks and Romans harvested the, then, limpid waters for sturgeon, tuna, gilt-head bream, mullet, sole, oysters, mussels, octopus and cuttlefish, in short all the fruit of the sea that we enjoy today; images of which they captured for eternity in the glittering mosaics of Pompeii and the *forum piscarium* of Rome.

Fish was not offered to the pagan gods, indeed the followers of Isis were forbidden to eat it, but it was a symbol and an important food for Roman Christians. Recently, an eminent Egyptologist friend expounded to me the enchanting premise that Christians used a fish as their symbol because, unlike their rivals the devotees of Isis, the fish was not forbidden to them. The Roman Catholic custom of eating fish on Fridays has, of course, been one of the major guiding reins on the long history of Italian food. The earliest cookery manuals are full of feast and fast day dishes and enormous effort and ingenuity was used to make fast day, *magra*, meals flavourful and interesting.

Living far from the sea in Italy makes buying snapping fresh fish difficult, however, many inland restaurants, including *pizzerie*, have regular supplies of fresh fish and shellfish rushed to them at the end of the week for the traditional Friday dishes. Some restaurants even have their own fishing boats and pride themselves on having fresh fish every day.

Italians tend to treat fish simply, serving it grilled or fried with a dusting of flour in a *fritto misto del mare*, which will include red mullet, squid and very often shrimp. There are also wonderful fish stews, sometimes flavoured with tomato and *peperoncino*, sometimes with black olives and parsley. These stews, called by different names on the varying coasts of Italy – in Apulia *brodetto*, along the Tuscan coast *cacciucco* – descend from the time when part of the peninsula was peopled by the Hellenes. Large fish, with the exception of canned tuna, do not go into pizza but there are some pizza recipes that make good use of shellfish, squid and of course anchovies. The 19th-century Neapolitan *pizzaioli* used preserved anchovies to economize on salt, and a popular pizza was garnished with *cecinielli*, tiny larval anchovies and sardines.

Very little fresh tuna is still caught in Italian waters, the small quantity due to over-fishing and pollution of the water; and what there is is difficult to obtain as a great deal of the catch is exported directly to Japan where it is greatly prized. So, Italians often buy their canned tuna at their local *pizzicheria*, once a pork butcher but now a sort of superior delicatessen. There it is sold from extremely large cans from which one buys sufficient for the dish in mind. The cans are usually kept behind the counter and are covered with white muslin. When bought in this way the tuna breaks up into large juicy pieces and is preserved in good quality olive oil. It is also possible, of course, to buy small cans of the fish preserved either in olive oil or brine; if possible buy *ventresca*, which is the middle cut and comes in larger chunks, and choose a can imported from Italy.

Italians very often buy their anchovies from large cans similar to those from which tuna is sold, but they are also available in small cans or glass jars. Always buy anchovies preserved in olive oil and use them all immediately, as once the jar is open they soon lose their freshness.

There are particular problems with using shellfish in *pizze*, as their delicate flesh becomes tough and inedible if exposed to too high and prolonged a heat. In professional pizzeria ovens the heat is so intense that a pizza will cook in four minutes, so they are able to put the raw shellfish on the dough and cook both together to perfection. When using a normal domestic oven it is better to add the shellfish to the pizza after it is cooked rather than risk spoiling their texture.

Notice that a pizza with fish or shellfish in the ingredients never includes cheese. Similarly, Italians do not serve parmesan to sprinkle over dishes of pasta that have shellfish or fish in the sauce, unless the sauce also contains other dairy products like cream or butter.

Pizzette con Le Cozze
Pizzette with Mussels

mussels
white wine
parsley
red chilli
  pepper
garlic
olive oil

When making a *Pizza con Le Cozze*, I like to cook the dough rapidly under an extremely hot grill. In this way the pizza crust remains soft and pliable. The mussels are cooked separately and added to the hot bread just before it is served.

To make two 6 inch pizzette you will need sufficient dough made according to the recipe on page 29 (about half the quantity given there); 12 to 15 mussels; ¼ pint/generous ½ cup/150 ml of dry white wine; 2 sprigs of parsley, chopped roughly with half a dried red chilli pepper. For the dough you will also need 2 tablespoons of vergine olive oil; 1 large clove of garlic, crushed and chopped; some coarse salt and freshly ground black pepper.

Scrub and beard the mussels under running water, rejecting any that are broken or open. Place them in a large saucepan with the wine, parsley and chilli pepper. Cover and cook the mussels over a low heat until they are all open, about five minutes. Drain the mussels, leaving them in their shells, and reserve the liquid. Keep both hot.

Meanwhile, heating up your grill to its absolute maximum capacity, roll out the dough into two small circles about six inches in diameter and about a quarter of an inch thick, and let them prove. Two small circles are easier to manipulate than one large one. As soon as the grill is vibrant with heat put the dough circles on the rack in the grill pan and place it as near the heat as possible. Let the dough cook for two to three minutes until the surface has whitened and is beginning to show dark brown spots of burning.

Remove the grill pan and with a fork or tongs turn over the circles, then quickly splash on the olive oil, scatter the chopped garlic, add the salt and replace the circles under the grill for a further two to three minutes or until they are beginning to scorch in patches.

When the circles are done, put them on serving plates and splash on some of the reserved mussel juice and a grind of black pepper. Arrange the hot mussels on the crust and serve immediately. I like to have some of the mussel liquid in a small bowl so that I can tear off pieces of the soft crust and dip them into the hot savoury juice.

Pizza con I Frutti di Mare
Seafood Pizza

To make a Pizza con I Frutti di Mare *you will need, as always, sufficient dough to provide a medium-size pizza base made from the recipe on page 29; 8 oz/1 cup/240 g tomato pulp (see page 52); 1 tablespoon of chopped parsley; salt and black pepper; 2 tablespoons of olive oil. Then, a mixture of diverse shellfish, perhaps 4 or 5 large mussels, about 10 clams in their shells, 3 or 4 large unshelled Dublin Bay prawns (saltwater crayfish), in short, whatever your fishmonger can provide. Finally you will need a little white wine, a little more olive oil and butter, and another 2 tablespoons of chopped parsley mixed with a finely chopped large clove of crisp garlic. Oven temperature: 425°F/220°C/7.*

mussels
clams
Dublin Bay
  prawns
  (saltwater
  crayfish)
tomato pulp
garlic
parsley
olive oil

Have the oven heating while you roll out the dough into a circle and put it on an oiled round pizza tin to prove or rise. Spread the tomato pulp over the proved dough, sprinkle on the parsley, salt and black pepper and trickle on the olive oil.

Put the pizza on the middle shelf of the oven and bake for fifteen minutes. It is best to cook the shellfish, but barely cook them, for this seafood pizza during the time that the pizza is baking, as then they will be fresh from the saucepan to immediately decorate the top of the crust.

Scrub and beard the mussels under running water, rejecting any that are broken or open. Place them in a large saucepan with a little wine. Cover and cook over a low heat until they are all open, about five minutes. Drain the mussels, leaving them in their shells. Keep warm.

Meanwhile, put the washed clams into a pan with one tablespoon olive oil. Cover and cook over a low heat until the clams are all open, then immediately drain and keep warm. To cook the prawns, warm one tablespoon of butter in a sauté pan and toss the prawns over medium heat until they change colour.

When the pizza is cooked take it from the oven and arrange upon it the hot cooked shellfish and prawns; sprinkle them liberally with the rest of the parsley and garlic and return the pizza to the oven for a further two to three minutes, no longer or the shellfish will become tough and inedible. These few minutes in the oven will give the sea shells a hot, baked, feel to them, an effect achieved with greater ease in a professional pizza maker's oven. The superior heat of these ovens will bake the raw shellfish *and* the crust in four to five minutes. Serve the pizza immediately when it is very hot.

Pizza con Le Vongole
Pizza with Clams

clams
tomato pulp
parsley
red chilli
  pepper
olive oil

Besides sufficient dough to make a medium-size base (see page 29) you will need 14 to 16 oz/400 to 450 g of clams in their shells; 3 tablespoons of extra vergine olive oil; 8 oz/1 cup/240 g of tomatoes, skinned, seeded and chopped, or the same quantity of tomato pulp (see page 52); salt and freshly milled black pepper; a few sprigs of parsley and a small piece of dried red chilli pepper – chop the chilli together with enough parsley to make up 1 tablespoon. Oven temperature: 425°F/220°C/7.

Put the washed clams into a saucepan containing one tablespoon of olive oil. Put on the lid and let the clams cook over a low heat until they are all open. As soon as this has happened drain off the small amount of liquid in the saucepan and put it into a bowl. Shell most of the clams, put the flesh into the bowl of liquid and leave in a warm place. Keep back about ten to twelve clams still in their shells.

Meanwhile have the oven heating up. Roll out the disc of dough and let it rest on a lightly oiled pizza tin or floured peel if you are baking on tiles. When the oven is hot put the tomato mixture on the dough, spreading it evenly over the surface, sprinkle on a seasoning of salt and black pepper and the two remaining tablespoons of olive oil. Consign the pizza to the oven and bake it for about fifteen to twenty minutes until the crust is golden.

Just before serving the pizza, scoop up the clams with a slotted spoon and sprinkle them over the tomato. Take the clams still in their shells and arrange them here and there on top. Sprinkle on the parsley and chilli mixture and if the tomato looks on the dry side dash on a little of the clam juice too.

Elegant macelleria in Bologna

Winter greens and oranges in Arezzo market

Pizza con Il Tonno e Cipolle
Pizza with Tuna and Onion

Tuna has a rich sweet flavour and makes an excellent ingredient for a pizza, especially when it is sparked off with a little crisp raw onion.

tuna
onion
capers
olive oil

You will need sufficient dough to make one medium-size pizza base as given in the recipe on page 29; a 6 or 7 oz/170 to 200 g can of Italian tuna fish, preferably preserved in olive oil; 1 small onion, if possible the ruby pink variety as it will add to the appearance of the pizza; 1 tablespoon of well-drained capers; salt and freshly ground black pepper; 2 tablespoons of extra vergine *olive oil. Oven temperature: 425°F/220°C/7.*

While the oven is heating to the correct temperature, roll out the disc of dough and let it prove or rise on the lightly oiled pizza tin or floured peel. Drain the tuna well of excess oil and especially well if it is preserved in brine. When the oven is hot, break the fish up into small pieces and spread them evenly over the surface of the dough.

Chip the onion into small slim half-moon shapes; do this by chipping away at the onion all around it rather than by chopping it into dice in the conventional manner. Sprinkle the onion pieces on top of the fish. Scatter the capers here and there, and add a sprinkling of salt and a little black pepper. Finally dribble on a generous two tablespoons of olive oil to ensure that the tuna does not dry out.

Bake the pizza for fifteen to twenty minutes. When the pizza crust is an appetizing gold and the oil sizzles it will be time to remove the dish from the oven and serve it immediately.

Pizza col Tonno e Pomodoro
Pizza with Tuna and Tomato

In this recipe the tuna is moistened by the addition of a layer of tomato. Use if you can ripe fresh tomatoes, deprived of their skins and chopped, as these will give a fresh taste to the pizza.

tuna
tomato pulp
black olives
olive oil

To make a medium-size round pizza you will need sufficient dough made from the recipe on page 29; 8 oz/1 cup/240 g of tomato pulp (see page 52); 6 oz/170 g can of good quality tuna fish, preferably preserved in olive oil, broken up into small pieces; 6 or 7 pitted black olives; salt and black pepper; 2 tablespoons of good green olive oil. Oven temperature: 425°F/220°C/7.

Have your oven heating up while you roll out the disc of dough and let it prove on a floured peel if you are going to bake the pizza on tiles, or on a flat oiled tin. When the oven is hot spread the tomato pulp evenly over the surface of the dough, leaving a border of about a quarter of an inch around the edge. On the tomato spread the tuna, scatter the olives here and there over the surface, and add a sprinkle of salt and a few turns of the pepper mill. Finally dribble on the olive oil and place the pizza in the hot oven. It will take about fifteen to twenty minutes to cook.

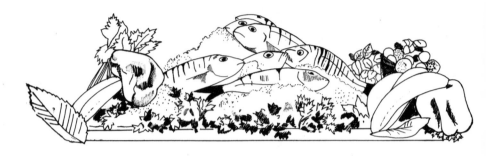

Pizza Rosa
Rose Pink Pizza

Dublin Bay
prawns
(saltwater
crayfish)
tomatoes
cream
parsley
olive oil

To make this very pretty pizza you will need sufficient dough for one medium-size base as given in the recipe on page 29; 4 large ripe tomatoes; 2 tablespoons of thin cream; salt and white pepper; 12 large raw Dublin Bay prawns (saltwater crayfish) in their shells; 1 tablespoon of finely chopped parsley; a little Ligurian or French olive oil. Oven temperature: 425°F/220°C/7.

Roll out the circle of dough and place it on an oiled pizza tin or floured board to prove while you heat the oven.

Deprive the tomatoes of their skins by dipping them into boiling water, then cut them into pieces and remove all the seeds. Mix the flesh and the cream into a thick purée, then season with salt and freshly ground white pepper – white pepper is used to obviate black specks in the rosy purée.

When the oven is hot spread the purée on the dough and bake for fifteen minutes. At this point add the prawns to the top of the pizza and cook in the hot oven for two to three minutes just until they are a lively pink. Just before serving the pizza add the chopped parsley and a little delicate olive oil.

I CALZONI
FOLDED PIZZA

Calzone is an Italian street word for trousers, and a word that is also used to describe a folded pizza, like a sealed pasty. The dough encloses the filling rather, I suppose, as buttoned breeches wrap around and enclose legs. There are various sorts of traditional fillings for *calzoni*, using chopped chard leaves or beet greens, and ricotta cheese. It is also possible to use cooked fish like fresh sardines or shellfish. However, the fillings that to my taste are most successful are those that include a large helping of mozzarella; the baked case when sliced open reveals the creamy mass of melted cheese sparked off with a few stronger tasting ingredients, the soft interior contrasting well with the crisp crust and giving a more satisfactory texture to the dish. The Italian *calzone* has been adapted by Alice Waters in her restaurant Chez Panisse in Berkeley, California. Using a mixture of her local Sonoma goat cheese, French goat cheese and mozzarella, with *prosciutto* and various fresh herbs, she has given brilliant new life to a traditional Italian recipe.

Drier *calzoni* fillings containing mixtures of sautéed vegetables are better when balanced with a fresh tomato sauce poured over the hot *calzone* just before it is served. You may, instead, pour on a measure of your best olive oil, which will moisten the baked dough and give it a wonderfully creamy texture and soft taste. Exercise your imagination and personal preferences and fill *calzoni* with all sorts of delicious ingredients. The main thing to remember is not to make the filling too wet or it will make the dough soggy and difficult to handle nor so dry as to make the texture of the *calzone* dull. Cheese that is solid when cold and soft when hot is an ideal answer. Mild gorgonzola with a little crisp raw onion might make good companions and wild *funghi* like chanterelles with mozzarella cheese would make a subtle filling. Very many of the seasonings suggested for open *pizze* would also be delicious in a *calzone*. The following recipes are ones that are commonly served in Italian *pizzerie* and are very popular.

Calzoni make a convenient way of cooking two servings at once on the same oven shelf. The master dough recipe on page 29 will produce sufficient to make two *calzoni* which, when folded, will take up the space of one round pizza in the oven.

Calzoni con Mozzarella e Prosciutto
Folded Pizza with Mozzarella and Parma Ham

mozzarella
prosciutto or
    cooked ham
preserved
    artichoke
    hearts
olive oil

To fill 2 calzoni *you will need* all *the dough made in the recipe on page 29; 3 tablespoons of olive oil; 12 oz/2 cups/340 g of mozzarella; 2 large slices of* prosciutto *or excellent quality cooked ham; 2 large preserved artichoke hearts (see page 79); salt and freshly milled black pepper. Oven temperature: 425°F/220°C/7.*

While the oven is heating up roll out the dough into two eleven inch circles. Leave on a floured surface to rest. Lightly oil a flat pizza tin or have tiles heating up in the oven if you prefer to bake on them.

When the oven is hot start to dress the *calzoni*. On to each circle paint one tablespoon of the olive oil, taking the oil right up to the edges.

Cut the mozzarella into large cubes and arrange an equal amount on each *calzone* but confine the filling to half the circle of dough and leave a small border at the outer edges.

Roll the slices of ham into tubes and put them on top of the cheese, one roll for each *calzone*. Split the artichoke hearts into halves and add them to each pile of stuffing. Sprinkle on a little salt and a generous amount of black pepper.

Now, fold the empty side of the dough over the filling so that the semi-circular edges come together and form a half-moon shape. Make sure the edges are well sealed by folding the dough over a little and pinching the edge. The stuffing should not escape during the cooking.

Paint the rest of the olive oil over the surface of the *calzoni* then carefully slide them on to the pizza tin or on to a floured peel, from which you may slide them on to the hot tiles. Watch to see that the dough does not split with the weight of the stuffing. Put them in the oven and let them cook for twenty minutes, until the crust is golden.

Serve them immediately with a fresh tomato sauce (see page 52) or green *extra vergine olio d'oliva*.

Calzoni con Le Salsicce
Folded Pizza with Sausages

To make 2 calzoni *you will need all the dough produced with the recipe on page 29; 12 oz/2 cups/340 g of mozzarella; 4 fresh pork sausages (see page 67 for details); 3 tablespoons of olive oil; salt and a little chopped hot red* peperoncino, *or red pepper flakes. Oven temperature: 425°F/220°C/7.*

mozzarella
fresh pork
  sausages
red chilli
  peppers
olive oil

Have your oven heating up while you roll out the dough into two eleven inch circles and let them rest on a floured surface. Cut the mozzarella into large chunks, remove the skins from the sausages and crumble up the meat with your fingers.

When the oven is hot start to dress the *calzoni*. First paint on two tablespoons of the olive oil all over the surface of the circles, then arrange the chunks of mozzarella on one half of each circle leaving a small border at the outer edges. Sprinkle the sausagemeat over the mozzarella, and add a little salt and a spray of chopped *peperoncino* or red pepper flakes. Next fold the empty side of the dough over the filling and press the edges together; turn the edges of dough over and pinch them to make a firm join.

Paint the rest of the olive oil over the two closed *calzoni* and carefully lift them on to the oiled pizza tin or on to a floured peel with which you may slide them on to the hot tiles. Cook the *calzoni* for twenty minutes.

Serve the *calzoni* hot from the oven accompanied by a fresh tomato sauce (see page 52) or green olive oil.

PASTE FRITTE
FRIED PIZZA

Today is the Feast of St. Joseph, the patron saint of all *frittaruoli*, or pastry cooks, using the word 'pastry' in its crudest sense. Since, under the black, boiling oil they use for frying, there is a constant flare of flame, all fiery torments are assigned to their mystery. Last night they decorated their house fronts with appropriate paintings: Souls in Purgatory and Last Judgements were blazing on all sides. In front of their doors large frying pans stood on hastily erected stoves. One apprentice kneaded the dough while a second shaped it into crullers and threw them into the boiling oil. A third stood beside the pan with a small skewer, picked out the crullers when they were cooked and put them on another skewer, held by a fourth apprentice, who then offered them to the bystanders. The third and fourth apprentices were young boys wearing blond, elaborately curled wigs, which are regarded as the attribute of angels. To complete the group, there were some persons who handed wine to the cooks, drank themselves and cried their wares. Angels, cooks, everybody shouted at the top of their voices. They drew a great crowd because, on this night, all pastry goods are sold at greatly reduced prices and even a portion of the profits is given to the poor.

Goethe *Italian Journey*

This is how Goethe described the noisy, lively Neapolitan feasts in 18th-century Naples, and these simple fritters prepared by the *frittaruoli* were the forebears of delicious modern *calzoncelli* and *pizzelle fritte*. In the Naples of the 1850s on the Feast of St. Joseph the round morsels of dough called by that time *zeppole* were still eaten by all Neapolitans.

At that time in every street as in every kitchen one sees nothing but great pans of boiling oil sitting on flaming stoves, pans in which the pale *zeppole* are fried.

Emmanuele Rocco
Usi e Costumi di Napoli e Contorni

In the country kitchen the most basic fried breads started with simple household bread dough left after the week's baking. The scraps of dough were rolled out, cut into strips or fingers and fried in boiling oil until they were puffed up and golden, to be eaten either sprinkled with salt as a change from ordinary bread or dipped in sugar as a simple treat. They have local names all over Italy. In parts of Tuscany they are called *frittelle, ficattole* or *donzelline*, in Umbria *tortucce* or *arvolte*. In Naples they are made from *pasta cresciuta*, which is a very soft, almost batter-like leavened dough. Sometimes housewives knead small quantities of rosemary or little pieces of cheese or *prosciutto* into the dough before shaping it into circles or diamonds and frying them; among these are the Bolognese *crescentini*. They all make excellent little savouries to eat with crudités, cheese or *prosciutto*.

Pizzelle fritte are delicious members of the pizza family: they are small rounds of dough which are first covered with various ingredients, such as mozzarella and anchovies, mozzarella and tomato or artichoke, or ricotta, *prosciutto* and parsley, then folded into semi-circles like *calzoni*. When the *pizzelle* are sealed they are fried in oil until golden, and make excellent luncheon dishes. *Calzoncelli* are very similar but they tend to have a soft filling bound together with beaten egg. *Panzarotti*, another small folded type of pizza, are daintier and are made from a much more refined unleavened dough.

Panzarotti often find a place in a *fritto misto alla Napoletana*, which is the Neapolitan version of one of Italy's great showpiece dishes, *I Grandi Fritti*. Here a great variety of ingredients are fried and served together on a large dish garnished with fresh lemon slices. The composition of various *grandi fritti* differ regionally in detail, but whether the *frittura* is *Milanese, Napoletana, Fiorentina, Romana* or *Emiliana* there are always four basic elements, sweetbreads, brains, bone marrow and artichokes. The additions can be liver, kidney, heart, cauliflowers, courgettes, courgette flowers, tomatoes, even Brussels sprouts, then various croquettes, cheeses, *supplí, bigné* and *panzarotti*.

Ficattole
Fried Dough

This is a good way to use up spare dough left after pizza or bread making. Knead the dough for a minute or so then roll it out into a sheet a little less than a quarter of an inch thick. With a sharp knife cut strips about four inches by three-quarters of an inch in size and make a slash with the knife through the length of each strip. Fry the *ficattole* in boiling sunflower or arachide oil a few at a time until they are swollen and golden. Drain them on kitchen paper and serve them hot and salt-sprinkled to accompany an antipasto of *prosciutto* and *salame* or crudités. A bottle of crisp white wine will not go amiss.

Delicious variations on this simple theme can be made by kneading into the basic dough little additions such as parmesan cut into tiny dice, or a few scraps of *prosciutto*, maybe a small sprig of tender new rosemary chopped into small pieces, or a few fresh sage leaves similarly sliced into shreds.

Calzoncelli
Small Fried *Pizze*

mozzarella
prosciutto
mortadella
tomato sauce
parmesan
parsley
basil
egg
oil for frying
tomato sauce for
  serving

To make 12 calzoncelli *you will need* all *the dough given in the recipe on page 29; 6 oz/1 cup/170 g of mozzarella; 2 slices of lean prosciutto; 2 small slices or 1 large of mortadella; 2 sprigs of parsley; 6 basil leaves; 3 tablespoons of freshly grated parmesan; a pinch of salt and freshly ground black pepper; 1 egg; 8 oz/1 cup/240 g of tomato sauce (see page 52); sunflower or arachide oil for frying.*

Cut the mozzarella into tiny dice, slice the *prosciutto* and mortadella into fine fragments, and chop the parsley and basil minutely together. Mix all these in a bowl with the parmesan, salt and pepper, and bind the mixture with the beaten egg. You should end up with a soft mass.

Divide the dough into twelve equal parts and roll each ball out into a circle about four inches in diameter and a sixteenth of an inch thick. Put a spoonful of filling on one side of each circle and fold the remaining dough over the filling to form small half-moon shapes. Seal the edges well by folding and pinching the dough.

Have the basil-flavoured tomato sauce ready to serve, and a steep-sided frying pan with about an inch of oil heating within it. When the oil bubbles when you flick some flour into it, add the *calzoncelli*, a few at a time. When they have puffed up and become golden on both sides, remove them to a hot plate covered with kitchen paper to blot off the excess oil.

Take them to the table while they are hot, so that the mozzarella in them is still soft and melted, and serve the sauce in a tureen so that those who enjoy it may help themselves.

Pizzelle Fritte
Simple Fried *Pizze*

The way of preparing and cooking these little *pizze* is identical to the last recipe for *calzoncelli*, that is rolling out the dough into small circles, adding the filling, folding over the dough and sealing it to make semi-circular turnovers; then frying them until they are golden brown in hot oil. The fillings for the *pizzelle* are, however, more simple – just two or three complimentary ingredients seasoned with salt and pepper.

Here are some suggestions for and quantities of ingredients

that will fill twelve *pizzelle*, made from *all* the dough produced from the recipe on page 29.

Mozzarella ed Acciughe *Mozzarella and Anchovies*

8 oz/1½ cups/240 g of mozzarella; 6 anchovy fillets; salt and pepper; 2 tablespoons of olive oil.

mozzarella
anchovies
olive oil

Dice the mozzarella and divide the cubes between each *pizzelle*, then add half an anchovy fillet, salt and pepper, and a dribble of olive oil to each one. Fold over and seal the *pizzelle* and cook them according to the instructions for *calzoncelli* opposite. Serve with a light tomato sauce as given on page 52.

Pomodoro e Basilico *Tomato and Basil*

4 oz/¾ cup/100 g of mozzarella; 6 tablespoons of tomato pulp (see page 52); 12 fresh basil leaves; salt and black pepper.

mozzarella
tomato pulp
basil

Dice the mozzarella and divide it up between the twelve circles of dough. Add half a tablespoon of tomato pulp to each, then one basil leaf, a sprinkle of salt and a turn of the pepper mill. Fold and seal the *pizzelle* and fry in hot oil according to the instructions opposite.

Mozzarella e Gorgonzola *Mozzarella and Gorgonzola*

4 oz/¾ cup/100 g of mozzarella; 4 oz/¾ cup/100 g of gorgonzola dolce (mild); salt and black pepper.

mozzarella
gorgonzola

Dice both the cheeses and mix them together; divide between the twelve *pizzelle* and season with a little salt and pepper. Fold up and seal the dough. Fry in hot oil according to the instructions opposite.

LA PIZZERIA
THE ITALIAN PIZZERIA

Since the first permanent pizzeria was opened at the Port Alba in Naples in 1830 an immense mountain of dough has been kneaded and countless *pizze* baked and enjoyed. Pizza was an essential part of the street life of Naples. But it was not until the middle years of our century that the Neapolitan notion of the pizzeria took hold and spread to northern Italy; taken out of its cradle by Neapolitans working in Rome and the industrial north who missed the easy pleasure of the Neapolitan pizzeria, the marble-topped tables, the flower sellers, the sounds of a mandoline and the taste of the fresh-baked crust. Today pizza is to be found in every Italian town and city.

Still, in Naples, one can eat at venerable *pizzerie*, sit at marble tables and be serenaded with sweet songs, and the pizza will not only contain good and genuine ingredients but will be made with spirit, a spirit of love and enthusiasm.

In an unprepossessing street, the Via Pietro Colletta which runs off the Corso Umberto I, you can buy what many Neapolitans agree is the best pizza in the world. The pizzeria is old and tiny and it is called the 'Pizzeria Trianon da Ciro'. When you step into the shop you are confronted by the fiery oven which nearly fills the room. It is large and beehive-shaped and covered in tiny white tesserae; a simple elegant T for Trianon is picked out in red above the oven's mouth. There is a small banquette of cool marble where the *pizze* are stretched into shape and bowls, holding the seasonings, stand in rows on small glass shelves. The two small dining rooms are clad to waist height in grey streaked marble as were all the old Neapolitan *pizzerie*. The pale grey painted upper walls have stucco friezes of fruit picked out in their natural colours. A large mirror is signed 'da Ciro'. The tables are marble-topped.

The clientèle are ordinary people from the quarter, which is not a rich one. They and their forebears have been eating the sort of pizza made here since the early years of the last century. Here you can find *real* Neapolitan pizza, Porcaro's 'divine food' 'made by the artistic hands of a Neapolitan *pizzaiolo*'. The *pizze* are large, light as a zephyr, and sing with rich saturated colour that is matched by the intensity of the flavour. The *quattro stagione* is divided by twists of dough to separate the tiny purple olives, the parsley and the anchovies, the miniature wild mushrooms with mint, and the mozzarella made from *latte di bufala*.

The style of the Trianon is simple. No places are set on the square marble tables; instead you are presented with a plate holding glasses and cutlery laid on a pile of newsprint squares which serve as napkins. Salt is provided in a cardboard salt packet standing on a ledge beneath the mirror; those who need it may reach across and help themselves.

The *pizze* when brought to the table are like jewels. Created from flour, yeast and water, decorated with a sure touch, they are as the Neapolitan writer Guiseppe Porcaro describes them: ' . . . round like the dazzling sun, soft and rosy like the chubby face of a doll, shining with the brilliance of a pomegranate seed, red like the carmine lips of a languid and voluptuous woman'. The simplest ingredients transformed into a brimming plate full of magic.

A small man, malformed and very near blind, comes to the pizzeria and sings, and the notes that come from his throat are of a piercing purity, a tenor soft and high and melodious. Every note contains six more. He sings a Neapolitan song about pizza.

From these sweet beginnings, the core of the world of pizza, still to be enjoyed in Naples, pizza has travelled and taken on the personality of new regions, their culinary traditions and particular ingredients. Only a short drive down the coast from Naples is a famous establishment, Gigino's 'Pizza al Metro' in Vico Equense. From the outside his pizzeria looks like a rather ordinary Italian family restaurant, a large one that can cater for weddings and first communion celebrations with ease; indeed the restaurant is usually full of noisy parties until the early hours. To enter the spacious high-ceilinged dining room you first have to step into the part of the kitchen where the pizza is made, and which is divided off from the eager customers by a long counter. Behind this are the *pizzaioli*, the pizza bakers. There at the back of the room all in a row lining the wall are five or so large wood-fired ovens glowing with heat. The air is thick with the scent of *pizze* cooking. Long wooden tables are loaded with balls of dough and large bowls of the myriad ingredients that are generously piled on to the *pizze*. Heaps of soft creamy mozzarella and *fior di latte* are cut into cubes by young assistants. Shiny black olives from Gaeta gleam in their white china bowls next to the scarlet sun-ripened plum tomatoes, dusty green oregano and fat fresh basil leaves. There are heaps of delicately sliced small mushrooms shaved fine at lightning speed by the sharpest of flashing knives. Speed is essential to feed the throng that come each day and most of the night.

The pizza bakers, swarthy young men dressed in white cotton, their brown arms dusted with flour, dart and weave with their long-handled *pale* with which they plunge the individual *pizze* into the fiery ovens and then retrieve them at the precise point in the cooking when the edge of the crust, the *cornicione*, is golden and swollen and starting to show patches of brown-black burning. Then with graceful skill they slip them on to plates to be sent scalding to the table.

As the name of the pizzeria suggests, you are not confined to ordering a normal round pizza. Here you may ask for a pizza up to a metre in length and it will be served sliced into generous oblong portions. This is not such an extravagantly greedy idea as it may seem as southern families tend to be large and when they venture out to celebrate they go *en famille* or in large groups of friends. In Rome one can also see large long *pizze* laid out on wooden planks. Garnished with their characteristic exuberance, the Roman *Margherita* has thick layers of soft red tomato decorated with bunches of fresh basil leaves that are unscorched by the oven's heat. And to contrast with the cooked tomato are clusters of tiny red cherry tomatoes arranged between the basil.

The essence of pizza is gaiety, *allegria*; most *pizzerie* have something special, something different to offer.

One of the liveliest and most popular *pizzerie* that I know is in Citta di Castello, a small Umbrian town in the plain of the Upper Tiber, not far from where Pliny the Younger had his Tuscan villa. It is called 'Adriano Due' and is run with great style by Adriano Chiarioni. During the span of his career he has seen the spread of the pizzeria through Italy, from the time when his parent's restaurant near Milan was transformed in the early 1950s into one of the first *pizzerie* to exist outside Naples. Adriano Due is a very good example of what a modern pizzeria can be when transplanted from its native soil and directed by an Italian from another area of Italy who adds his own attributes and tastes to the original concept.

Adriano, even as a small boy, always knew what he wanted to be when he grew up; a restaurateur. He grew up in the atmosphere of his family's business, learnt to serve at table and to love good food. Eager to have wider experience in his chosen profession the young Adriano became an apprentice at the famous and luxurious restaurant 'Savini' in the *Galeria* at Milan; it was there that he acquired his style.

He becomes quite nostalgic when remembering the beautiful way in which the tables were arranged at Savini's, with heavy padded cloths laid first to deaden the sound of the plates and cutlery, the immaculate linen tablecloths, heavy solid silverware, crystal narrow-stemmed drinking glasses and fine china. It was there that he was taught by stern elderly waiters how to serve a fresh peach correctly. How, in front of the client, you would peel it with a knife and fork and then cut it into delicate petals until there remained a soft rose shape on the plate.

Today, Adriano sees his pizzeria as a place, unlike a formal restaurant, where people can come and be free in their choice of meal. They do not have to sit through a conventional Italian meal of antipasto, pasta, meat or fish course, *contorno*, the vegetable course, dessert and coffee; although he is very happy to serve just that if the customer so wishes. A pizza is a *piatto unico*, a meal in itself, and it is as cheap and nourishing as ever it was in 19th-century Naples where it was designed to fill the hungry stomachs of the impecunious. But apart from giving sustenance, Adriano says that eating pizza fulfils a social role in Italian society. A group of friends will gather, someone will say '*andiamo mangiare un pizza*', and they will all pile into cars, drive to their favourite place and spend the time talking, drinking a little wine or beer from the barrel, now enormously popular, and just enjoy being together in pleasant surroundings, in the Italian version of the pub or local bar. It is not a seasonal activity, people go to *pizzerie* all year round; some go with their children early in the evening, others belong to the late, two-in-the-morning, crowd. For the young eating pizza has always been normal, but today older people are joining in. Adriano's clientèle has changed somewhat, the parents and grandparents of the young are discovering that it is fun to go out in a group, that it makes them feel livelier. They are no longer quite so conscious of the old small-town restrictions on their behaviour.

Adriano Due is to be found in the corner of a small square outside the ancient walls of Citta di Castello – any passer-by will direct you there. Its large windows are framed by cheerful yellow and white striped blinds and outside there are three or four tables which are pleasant to sit at on warm summer evenings. Inside, the restaurant is large and cool; as you enter there is a handsome wooden bar with comfortable stools where you can sit and drink one of Adriano's inimitable cocktails or a glass of chilled white wine before going to your table, which will be spread with a pale blue and yellow lily-patterned damask cloth of the kind that Italians design and weave so beautifully.

One of Adriano's specialities in land-locked Umbria is fish, brought fresh daily from the east coast; the black-trousered white-shirted waiters dart back and forwards with large bowls of steaming mussels and great platters of *pesce alla griglia*, made up of delicious red mullet, giant prawns, crayfish, sole, *coda di rospo* (angler fish tails) and whatever else happens to be fresh that day. The waiters also carry plates of bubbling, scorching pizza made by Guiseppe Lombardi, the reigning *pizzaiolo*.

Guiseppe comes from Citta di Castello and is a handsome, rather grave young man. He moves slowly and deliberately, dressing his *pizze* with calm delicacy. His corner of the restaurant is closed off from the main room by two waist-high walls, but it is in full view of anyone who cares to watch him at work. The walls are lined with palest green tiles and he has polished rose-granite coloured cool marble surfaces on which to spread the dough. He bakes in a round beehive-shaped vaulted oven set into the wall, and through its square opening you can see the brightly burning wood fire. On a long and busy evening he will need all of a *quintale* or 100 kilos of wood to maintain the right degree of heat.

Guiseppe started work as a waiter but became interested in baking. He was taught his job by another *pizzaiolo*, a Neapolitan, who has since left the restaurant. He learnt by watching and working with his colleague and in this way, it is my impression, the secrets of making pizza have spread by word of mouth and example right through Italy. There are many *pizzaioli* from the south who, wanting a change of scene, go from city to city as their fancy takes them, always able to ply a useful trade.

Guiseppe's long evenings start several hours before he bakes the first pizza of the night. He has to fire the oven which takes two hours to achieve the correct temperature. This is between 400° and 500°C and can get as high as 700°C, though this is too hot and will scorch the *pizze*. When the circular oven is cold, the bricks of which it is constructed are black. Guiseppe lights a fire with brush wood and small logs along the left-hand curve of the circular base, and, gradually, as the heat grows greater the black dome changes. Above the fire the bricks become white and this whiteness travels across the dark vault in a wave exactly like the sun rising and filling the sky with light. When the entire brick vault has a pearly tone the oven is hot enough for baking.

Meanwhile Guiseppe has been attending to his dough. On a normal weekday night he will need to use about seven to eight kilos of flour, on Saturdays maybe as much as thirteen kilos. He uses, as do all professional *pizzaioli*, the refined 00 flour, not the more robust 0 grade flour which is used for bread; this 00 flour, also used for cakes and pastries, gives a silkier, softer dough and produces a lighter pizza. (However, for domestic purposes with less efficient ovens it is best to stick to a more powerful flour.) For every two to three kilos of flour he will need one litre of water. The compressed yeast, which he buys in 500 gram blocks, he measures by eye, about a *pugno*, a fistful. Guiseppe measures everything, as do most Italian cooks, by eye, feel and experience. (Professional bread bakers are an exception, and weigh their ingredients.) Apart from these three basic items he adds salt and again by eye about a quarter of a litre of olive oil, not *extra vergine* oil but simple, honest *olio d'oliva*. This, he says, adds colour and improves the texture of the dough. To make up the dough, he pours the flour into the bowl of a large electric mixer, then he dissolves the yeast and the salt in cold water. This surprised me, being mindful of all the injunctions one has ever read as to the necessity of using warm water to bring the yeast to life. He adds the liquid to the flour, starts the mixing and lastly adds the olive oil.

His dough when kneaded takes two hours to rise, but before the dough is risen Guiseppe forms it into round, slightly flattened balls which weigh 150 grams each. He arranges these in rows in a series of wooden drawers which line the inside of his work counter. Over the dough he lays a damp muslin cloth. When he has an order for a pizza he will take one of the by now risen balls of dough and flatten it out with his hands on the flour-strewn cold marble surface. When the dough is flattened he picks it up with both hands and stretches it by holding his hands fingers outspread under the dough and pulling outwards. Then he lays the disc, about twelve inches in diameter, again on the marble, and flattens it once again. Thin *pizze* are now popular, more than the thick *cornicione* or outer rim of the Neapolitan variety, and Guiseppe's dough is about an eighth of an inch thick. The pizza is now ready to dress and his customers have a choice of twenty-four different varieties, plus *Pizza Fantasy* where they are enjoined to ask for whatever combination of flavours takes their fancy. When I asked Guiseppe which pizza was the most popular he replied without hesitation the *Quattro Stagione* and next the *Margherita*.

Ranged in front of Guiseppe on glass shelves are bowls of all the most commonly used ingredients, olives, capers, anchovies, button mushrooms and a massive bowl of tomato which is the basis for many, many *pizze*. The tomato mixture consists of *pelati*, that is canned peeled whole San Marzano tomatoes, chopped to break up large pieces and then mixed with olive oil, salt, black pepper and oregano. Guiseppe uses a large kitchen spoonful of this mixture for each pizza, which comes to about three or four tablespoons. He spreads it over the dough with the back of the spoon leaving just a narrow border. If he is making for example a *Capricciosa*, he will then add a handful of diced mozzarella, made from cow's milk, *latte di mucha*, rather than that of *bufala* which is now too rare and expensive, two handfuls of sliced mushrooms, three or four preserved artichokes and two thin slices of *prosciutto cotto* torn into pieces. All these ingredients being arranged he will dip his *pala*, his metal peel, into flour, scoop up the raw pizza and with an elegant flick place it on the stone floor of the hot oven to bake. He places the pizza on the side away from the fire but adjusts the position occasionally as the pizza cooks. The baking takes four to five minutes, and this brief period of cooking is what gives the professionally baked pizza an edge over what can be managed in a domestic oven. The dough rises and cooks rapidly and the dressing takes but that same time to become sizzlingly hot. The rapidity means that the dough does not have time to harden and become tough. To watch a good *pizzaiolo* removing a pizza from the searing oven and flicking it on to a plate with grace and ease before it is borne bubblingly hot to the table, is to see one of the most Italian of gestures.

Adriano Chiarioni does not only believe in freedom of choice for his customers but also for his cooks and his *pizzaiolo*. He encourages them to create new flavours and to try out diverse ideas, and together they produce original and fresh-tasting dishes. The following three recipes are examples of the sort of *pizze* that their customers enjoy.

Pizza Marcellina

tomato pulp
mozzarella
button
   mushrooms
black olives
egg
olive oil

Guiseppe and Adriano invented their *Pizza Marcellina* in honour of Guiseppe's wife. It makes clever use of a raw egg cloaked with other ingredients – by giving the egg a protective coating of cheese it is possible to prevent it becoming tough in the oven's heat.

To make this pizza you will need sufficient dough for one medium-size pizza base made according to the recipe on page 29; 1 very fresh egg; salt; 4 oz/¹⁄₂ cup/100 g tomato pulp (see page 52); 3 oz/generous ¹⁄₂ cup/80 g of finely sliced button mushrooms; 3 oz/¹⁄₂ cup/80 g of finely sliced mozzarella; 6 black olives; black pepper; 2 tablespoons of good olive oil. Oven temperature: 425°F/220°C/7.

While the oven is heating to the required temperature, roll out your disc of dough and place it on an oiled pizza tin to prove. When you are ready to bake, crack the egg on to the dough, if it is fresh the albumen will not be overly runny. Sprinkle a little salt on the egg white.

With a spoon add the tomato pulp around the egg, sprinkle the fine mushroom slices all over the pizza, then the sliced mozzarella – try and cover the egg without breaking the yolk. Add the olives where you please, add a little more salt and black pepper, and dribble on the olive oil. Consign the pizza to the hot oven and bake for fifteen to twenty minutes until the crust is golden and the cheese melted.

Ceccho's basket with schiacciata con salvia

Violet tinted artichokes

Pizza Contadina
Country Pizza

To make this country pizza you will need sufficient dough for one medium-size pizza base, made according to the recipe on page 29; 8 oz/1 cup/240 g of tomato pulp (see page 52); 4 oz/³⁄₄ cup/100 g of diced mozzarella; 3 oz/a generous ¹⁄₂ cup/80 g of finely sliced button mushrooms; 6 or 7 black olives; 2 plump Italian pure pork sausages (as a substitute use coarsely minced lean pork flavoured with salt, black pepper and a little garlic); salt and pepper; 2 tablespoons of olive oil. Oven temperature: 425°F/220°C/7.

tomato pulp
mozzarella
button
   mushrooms
fresh pork
   sausages
olives
olive oil

While the oven is heating, roll out the dough and let it prove or rise on an oiled pizza tin. When the oven is fully heated spread the tomato on the pizza then sprinkle on the cheese, mushrooms and olives. Split the sausages, discard the skins and crumble the meat on to the pizza, add salt and black pepper, and dribble on the olive oil. Bake for fifteen to twenty minutes until the crust is golden.

Pizza Adriano Due

This pizza contrasts the differing flavours and textures of raw and cooked ingredients.

tomato pulp
mozzarella
preserved
   artichokes
gorgonzola
olive oil

You will need sufficient dough for one medium-size pizza made according to the recipe on page 29; 8 oz/1 cup/240 g of tomato pulp (see page 52); 4 oz/³⁄₄ cup/120 g of diced mozzarella; 4 or 5 preserved artichoke hearts (see page 79); salt and freshly milled black pepper; 2 tablespoons of olive oil; 1 thin slice of fresh, creamy gorgonzola. Oven temperature: 425°F/220°C/7.

While the oven is heating, roll out your disc of dough and leave it to prove on an oiled pizza tin or on a floured peel if you wish to bake on tiles. When the oven is hot begin to dress the pizza.

First put on a layer of tomato pulp and on top of this sprinkle the mozzarella. Place the artichokes in a ring around the pizza, splitting them if they are too large. Add salt and black pepper and dribble on the olive oil.

Bake the pizza for fifteen to twenty minutes until the crust is golden, then, before taking it to the table, lay the slice of gorgonzola in the centre of the ring of artichokes.

Guiseppe's favourite *pizze* are those without mozzarella, which to him tends to hide other flavours. He enjoys the classic *Marinara*, which is made with tomato, garlic and olive oil (see page 45) and also *Pizza Frutti di Mare*, which he makes with a layer of *seppie in umido*, stewed cuttlefish, cooked in the restaurant's kitchen with a *sofritto* of onion, *peperoncino*, olive oil and white wine, to which he adds a decorative flower made up of raw mussels in their shells, prawns and *vongole*.

Guiseppe's version of *Pizza Frutti di Mare* is rich and savoury, quite unlike one that I ate once in Lodi, that pretty *ottocentesca* town just south of Milan with its elegant Italian art nouveau houses and wide piazza. There a spectacular creation arrived at the table, a plain pizza covered with a mass of different molluscs still steaming in their shells; it tasted of fresh bread and the sea. There were small grey clams, larger *vongole verace*, navy razor clams, a scallop or two with brilliant corals reflected in the rose of their inner shells, large scarlet-whiskered prawns and tiny black mussels: a small representation of the vivid fish markets of Italy.

As the pizza has settled in Umbria and Tuscany it has taken on shades of the personality of those regions. These are the areas where the women have always baked the hearthbreads, the *torta al testo* and *schiacciata* (see page 122). Now, in many *pizzerie* in the area, the *pizze* are baked by women, a job which has always been a male preserve in the urban south. The ingredients change too, in *funghi*-rich Umbria *pizze* are sometimes piled with velvety *porcini*, or cèpes.

Southern Italians from Naples and Palermo have moved north, bringing with them their own style and their recipes. Valentino Caldiero of 'La Toula', Via San Lorentino in the *centro storico* at Arezzo, came originally from Sicily where there is a great tradition of closed *pizze* called *sfinciuni*. He serves clever, interesting dishes like this *Caccione*, which is a delicious oregano-perfumed *calzone* filled with mozzarella and *prosciutto*, and on top of the baked crust he lays slices of fresh ripe tomato bathed with excellent Tuscan olive oil. Here you are presented with a subtle mixing of flavours, temperatures and textures; the contrast between the raw and the cooked. Valentino also makes a splendid *Pizza al Noci*, which consists of tomatoes and mozzarella abundantly sprinkled with walnuts. The nutty taste of the crust enhanced by the walnut flavour is excellent. However, his most distinguished pizza, a *sfinciuni*, you have to order specially on quiet evenings. This splendid dish, called *Lucciariello*, contains cooked broccoli mixed with crumbled Italian butcher's sausages finished in a pan with olive oil and *peperoncino*, which is then layered with fresh tomato, encased in two sheets of dough and baked in the oven. This extremely good closed pizza was awarded a medal at a competition in Palermo.

Caccione
The Gossip

Valentino named this *calzone* after the Italian word to chatter or gossip as a great many people when seeing it written on the menu are curious to know what it is, and are surprised by the raw tomato when it arrives at their table.

mozzarella
prosciutto
tomato
oregano
olive oil

To make 2 Caccione *you will need all the dough made from the recipe on page 29; 2 tablespoons of olive oil; 12 oz/2 cups/350 g of mozzarella; 2 slices of lean* prosciutto; *salt and freshly ground black pepper; a large pinch of aromatic dried oregano (see note on page 37), or if this is not available, thyme and a little chopped parsley; 2 large ripe and juicy tomatoes; extra olive oil as needed. Oven temperature: 425°F/220°C/7.*

Roll out the dough into two medium-size circles. Leave them to prove on a floured surface while the oven is heating. Paint the olive oil over the surface of the dough, then on one half of each circle, leaving a small border around the edge, place the mozzarella cut into cubes. Add the *prosciutto*, cut into wide strips, and season with salt, pepper and the oregano or thyme and parsley. Fold the bare side of each *calzone* over the stuffing to make a half-moon shaped pasty. Seal the edges by folding the dough over and pinching it tightly together. The filling must not escape when the pizza is baked.

Brush a little extra olive oil over the surface of the *calzoni* and put them on an oiled tin into the hot oven to bake for twenty minutes or until the crust is golden.

Just before serving the *calzoni* slice the tomatoes into thin rounds and lay them over the top of the crusts. Provide some excellent *extra vergine* olive oil, to pour over the *calzoni* before they are cut open to reveal the soft oregano-scented melting cheese.

Pizza al Noci
Pizza with Walnuts

This pizza is excellent in autumn when the soft new walnuts are just ripe.

tomato pulp
mozzarella
walnuts
olive oil

You will need enough dough to make one medium-size base, made from the recipe on page 29; 8 oz/1 cup/240 g of tomato pulp (see page 52); 3 oz/½ cup/80 g of mozzarella; black pepper; an abundant amount of shelled walnuts broken into pieces, about 15 whole nuts; 2 tablespoons of olive oil. Oven temperature: 425°F/220°C/7.

Roll out the dough into a circle and let it prove on an oiled pizza tin or floured board while the oven heats. When the oven is hot spread the tomato pulp on to the dough, add the mozzarella cut into small dice and season with black pepper. Add the broken walnuts and dribble on the olive oil. Bake the pizza for twenty minutes until the crust is golden.

Lucciariello
Broccoli and Sausage Pie

broccoli
fresh pork
  sausages
tomatoes
garlic
chilli pepper
olive oil

This delicious Sicilian closed pizza is a favourite of mine. It will be sufficient for four to six people.

You will need all *the dough from the recipe on page 29; 12 oz/300 g of broccoli; 4 tablespoons of olive oil; 2 cloves of garlic; 1* peperoncino, *a small hot red Jalapeno or chilli pepper; 4 Italian butcher's sausages or coarse-cut pork sausages, or the equivalent weight (about 4 oz/100 g) of ground pork seasoned with salt and ground black pepper; 2 large ripe tomatoes. Oven temperature: 425°F/220°C/7.*

Divide the dough into two portions, one slightly larger than the other. Roll out the larger piece into a twelve inch circle and let it prove or rise on a flat oiled pizza tin. Roll out the second piece into a slightly smaller circle and leave it on a floured work surface. Have the oven heating to the correct temperature.

Trim the broccoli and cook it in salted boiling water until it is almost tender, then drain and chop into pieces about the size of a small walnut. In a sauté or frying pan heat two tablespoons of the olive oil and in it warm the garlic, cut into slices, and the roughly chopped *peperoncino* plus its seeds. Do not let these burn. Add the broccoli pieces and turn them in the hot oil until they have absorbed the flavours.

In another pan heat another tablespoon of oil and in it gently brown the sausages, which you have first skinned and crumbled into small pieces. Mix the broccoli and the cooked sausage together, taste to check the seasoning and let the mixture cool.

Spread the cool filling over the larger circle of dough leaving a border around the edge. Skin and thinly slice the tomatoes and arrange them in a layer over the filling, then add a little salt and pepper. Take the smaller circle of dough and place it on top of the filling. Bring the edges of the lower circle of dough up and over the top circle, pinching them together to make a tight seal. Paint on the remaining olive oil and bake the *Lucciariello* in the hot oven for twenty to twenty-five minutes until the crust is golden and crisp.

SAVOURY
HEARTHBREADS

LE SCHIACCIATE, LE FOCACCE
FLAT HEARTHBREADS

Flat hearthbreads are venerable in their antiquity, they are the domestic branch of the pizza story and they still continue to be made today in various forms, whether in fragrant bakeries, by country firesides or in the exquisite *cucine componibili*, the interior-designed kitchens of the middle classes. The word *schiacciare* means to crush or flatten; *schiacce* are roughly flattened stones, and *schiacciata* or *ciaccia* is a form of flat bread properly cooked upon them.

Years ago in the houses of country dwellers the deep stone fireplace was the hub of the household, and this, before the advent of the *cucina economica* (a simple wood-burning stove), was where most of the food was cooked. A flat thin stone was kept behind the fire and this, remaining hot in the perpetually burning embers, was always at hand to prepare the hearthbread. *Schiacciata* as it is called in Tuscany and Umbria; *focaccia* in Liguria, a name deriving from *focus*, the Latin word for hearth. These breads have always been cooked by women, unlike the Neapolitan pizza which was an urban dish baked and sold by men to poor townspeople who had no hearths.

My neighbour Maddalena Beligni, Nena, talks with wry nostalgia about her life's work, the care of her family, the cooking and the baking over the open fire and in the bread oven. It is of course women like her who have unconsciously handed down the traditions, retracing the patterns of culture first laid down by the original natives of the peninsula, then by the Etruscans, Greeks and Romans.

Nena is a tiny bird-like woman with bright grey eyes, always dressed in her enveloping pinafore and her *fazzoletto*, a neat kerchief around her head. Although she was born in 1912 in a neighbouring village, she has lived nearly all her life in our remote valley. When her parents were still alive and their house packed with brothers and sisters and children, about twelve of them in all, she made the bread and *schiacciata* for all the family, two dozen one-kilo loaves at a time. She has, she says, kneaded enough dough, in her time, to fill the *pieve*, the parish church. Now she is a widow and lives with just her youngest son in a well-proportioned stone house high on the slopes of the valley, nearly at the forest's edge. It is a pleasant house that catches the last gleams of the evening sun after the rest of the valley is dark, and there are old roses and vines around the doors.

As there are just the two of them to feed Nena buys what bread they need from the baker's boy who comes in a van to outlying houses. But still in her large long kitchen there is an ample *madia*, a chest-like piece of furniture with a lidded bread trough on top and cupboards with doors beneath. In this *madia* she kneaded the flour, yeast and water to make their saltless daily bread; this was always done in the evening and the dough was left in the chest overnight to rise. Early in the morning she shaped the dough into long oval loaves which were laid on a rough floured cloth on a long plank to prove for two hours or so. Meanwhile she would light the fire in the domed bread oven which is always found in country houses; in Tuscany and Umbria it is usually placed under the stairs that lead up to the main door on the first floor. The fire she lit with a bundle of dry twigs for kindling and short logs, and it was arranged around the edge of the circular base of the oven. She could tell when the oven was hot enough by looking at the interior walls; if they were white then the oven was ready. She then brushed the oven floor with a reed brush to clear it of ash and cinders and she took the bread outside on the plank and placed it as quickly as possible in the oven with a long-handled paddle called a *pala*, exactly as *pizzaioli* do now in similar-shaped pizza ovens. Then a metal or wooden door was clamped over the oven mouth and the bread took about an hour to bake. Carrying the loaves outside on a hot summer's day was one thing, but, in the cold winter rain, quite another. Nena baked again when the two dozen loaves were all eaten.

Now, Nena is thankful that at her age she no longer has to bake in this way, though her bread, she says, was much better than what is available today. She buys, too, her *schiacciata*, which once she made on the hearthstone.

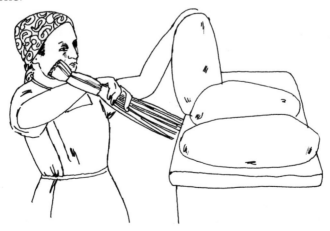

Originally, in far antiquity, the recipe for hearthbread, *panis focacius* or *subcinericus*, would have been extremely simple, like the kneaded meal of Cato, slapped on to hot stones and baked under a crock. My neighbour Silvana Cerotti still bakes her *schiacciata*, her *panis focacius*, over the open fire, using a slightly more modern version of the *schiacce* called a *pannaio*. I described this in my previous book, *The Tuscan Year*:

> . . . When she has a mind to bake the bread, she makes sure that the fire is burning brightly then goes to the pantry to find the *pannaio*. This is a round slab of heavy earthenware about fifteen inches in diameter and three inches thick. Growing out of the top is a ridge that serves as a handle: the *pannaio* is exceedingly heavy. These old-fashioned clay slabs are hard to find. Silvana bought hers from a very old man on the Umbrian side of the valley who is famous for his handiwork. Modern ones tend to be made of circular pieces of concrete with a thin metal handle embedded on one of the surfaces. She sets the *pannaio* right on the brightly burning fire to heat up.
>
> . . . When she is satisfied with the texture of the dough she wraps it in a clean cloth and returns to the kitchen to set it in a pan to rest in the warm stone cavity under the hearthstone. It will rest there for about half an hour and should increase to about twice its size.
>
> The *pannaio* becomes white hot, as it has to be to cook the bread. To test the heat Silvana sprinkles flour on to the stone: the flour browns immediately. She punches the risen dough into a rough circular shape and then slaps it on to the scalding stone; this needs practice. The next step is to prick the bread all over with a large fork. After a few minutes she puts a huge saucepan lid right over the *pannaio* and on top of this heaps glowing embers, which will serve to cook the top of the bread.
>
> *The Tuscan Year*

In Umbria the *pannaio* is called a *testo*, perhaps a connection between the *testu*, crock, used in Cato's simple recipe quoted at the very beginning of this book. Usually these *testi* come in the form of round slabs moulded from a type of aggregate with two handles embedded in the sides or one on the surface. The Umbrians call their simple homemade flat bread *torta al testo* and although they use the *pannaio/testo* in much the same manner as Silvana, the plain Umbrian *torta* contains only flour, a pinch of salt, a pinch of bicarbonate of soda and water. Of course there are also *torte condite*, breads enlivened with a variety of ingredients. The Umbrians do not cover the bread with a lid and hot ashes, but instead, when the lower side is cooked and crisp, they turn the cake over on the hot stone to bake both sides. The *torta* must be eaten hot from the fire and is usually served cut into wedges with *prosciutto*, *salame* or *verdura cotta*, cooked green-leaved vegetables.

There is still one place that I know of where it is possible for a passer-by to taste a genuine *ciaccia* made in the old-fashioned way. This is in the *Enoteca* in the main street of Tuscan Cortona; it is run by Imola Solfanelli Monacchini, the wife of the Mayor of Cortona. Here you may taste excellent Tuscan wines and eat extraordinarily good pecorino, *prosciutto* and Imola's famous bread. Imola comes from a *contadino* family who always baked their bread in their outdoor brick oven. She prepares the dough for the *ciaccia* the night before it is to be baked, using just flour, water and a sourdough yeast, by which I mean a piece of dough held back from the previous baking, the leaven always used in the past. The dough is given all night to rise, which allows the flavour to develop, then early the next morning it is kneaded again and allowed to rise a second time. After it is shaped into round flat loaves it is left to rise a third time and then it is baked in the outside oven that is fired with fragrant wood. Imola says that when she was a child the *ciaccia* was always put in to bake first, near to the oven's mouth; when it was done it meant that the oven was ready for the large loaves of bread. They ate the *ciaccia*, she says, split, sprinkled with their own olive oil and with ripe tomatoes, crushed between their fingers, spread on top. Her *schiacciata* is the best that I have ever eaten.

The Italian country women who made and still make these hearthbreads used their imaginations and whatever ingredients that came to hand to embellish an everyday bread and turn it into a special treat. In rural Britain bread dough was enhanced in similar ways too; but usually with spices and dried fruits to make wonderful sweet currant breads and yeast cakes, a subject which is beautifully treated by Elizabeth David in her *English Bread and Yeast Cookery*. The principle behind these household enriched breads remains the same: to produce something special out of very little. The Italians also have a tradition of making sweet cakes and breads, and until quite recently were not at all abashed by combining sweet and savoury elements together in the same dish. There are many recipes for cakes made of chestnut flour, spiced with rosemary and mixed with olive oil. The history of *panettone*, *pan dolce* and *panforte* is long and interesting, and is a branch of the history of seasoned breads, but must remain outside the scope of this book.

Schiacciate are simple and quick to make whether they are plain or enriched with savoury additions, and the recipes given further in this chapter make unusual and flavoursome breads to serve to guests or take on picnics. Two or three different types served together at a buffet supper are decorative and add interest to the table.

Schiacciata
Hearthbread

flour
yeast
sugar
olive oil
coarse salt

The following recipe for *schiacciata* will produce a fairly light round flat bread, somewhat akin to that baked in professional bakeries but still with the robust quality of a genuine home-made country hearthbread. The texture of the bread itself will be close and chewy, and is excellent whether eaten instead of bread, with a soup, or used to make sandwiches of *prosciutto*, *salame*, or perhaps some soft strachino cheese or fresh peco-rino.

To make an eleven to twelve inch round bread sufficient for 4 to 6 people you will need for the dough 10½ oz/3 cups/300 g of strong unbleached flour or American unbleached all-purpose flour; 1 heaped teaspoon of salt; ½ level teaspoon of active dried yeast gran-ules; ½ teaspoon of sugar; a generous 6 fl oz/¾ cup/175 ml of hand-hot water; 1 tablespoon of olive oil. To season the schiacciata *you will need 2 tablespoons of olive oil and a large pinch of salt – either coarse sea salt or Maldon salt, which is perfect for the purpose, crystalline but not rock-like to the tooth. Oven temperatures: 425°F/220°C/7; 400°F/200°C/6.*

Place the unsifted flour in a large warm mixing bowl, scatter in the salt and mix it through with a fork. Dissolve the yeast and the sugar in a little of the hand-hot water, and let the mixture stand for ten minutes until it creams and fizzes. Next make a well in the flour and pour in the yeast mixture and a generous tablespoon of olive oil. Start to mix the dough, pushing the flour down into the yeasty water; then add the rest of the water as it is needed. The dough for the *schiacciata* needs to be soft, *gommosa* as Italian women say, so make your mixture on the sticky side, controlling the dough with just a spoonful of extra flour if needed.

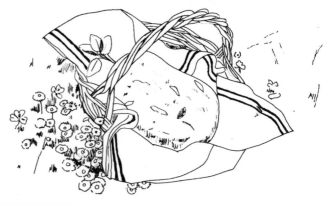

When the dough has come together put it on to a lightly floured board and knead it lightly for about ten minutes. Italians also say that *schiacciata* dough must not be over-handled, so use your fingers more than your palms and when sticky patches appear as you knead, dust them with the smallest amount of flour possible. You can manage a wet dough with surprisingly little extra flour. Roll the dough into a ball, make a cross cut with a sharp knife on the top to aid the rising, put it into a flour-sprinkled bowl, cover closely with a plastic bag and leave in a warm draught-free place to rise for about an hour.

Meanwhile lightly oil a flat round tin or oven sheet. When the dough has doubled in size knead it again very gently and then flatten it into a rough circle; handle the dough with delicacy. Put the circle on to the oiled tin and spread it with your palms into an eleven to twelve inch circle; the dough should be about half an inch thick and dimpled and uneven in its surface. Next take a wooden fork and make holes with its tines here and there over the *schiacciata*, then leave the tin aside, loosely covered, in a warm place – the table in a warm kitchen will do splendidly. This second rising will take about forty-five minutes and the dough should grow another half inch or so. Turn the oven to the first temperature setting in time for it to be fully hot before the bread is ready to bake.

When the oven is hot take a tablespoon or so of the olive oil and smear it with your fingers all over the surface of the dough – be generous, leaving small pools in the dimples. Then sprinkle on a little coarse salt.

Bake the bread on a middle shelf for fifteen minutes at the first setting, then turn the oven down to the second setting and bake for another five to ten minutes. The *schiacciata* will swell and become a light golden brown. After about twenty-five minutes of baking, remove it and cool it on a wire rack, then paint on a little more olive oil.

The surface of the *schiacciata* will have a crisp, slightly flaky texture from the oil, which will also give it a wonderful fruity flavour.

Schiacciata con Le Cipolle
Hearthbread Seasoned with Onion

Make the *schiacciata* exactly as is given in the previous master recipe. When you are ready to put the bread into the hot oven, instead of dressing it with simple oil and salt, use the following mixture.

dough
onion
sage or
    anchovies
olive oil

Slice a small white sweet onion into thin rounds, sprinkle these with salt and leave them aside until some of the onion liquid is drawn out. Rinse the excess salt away and pat the onion rings dry with kitchen paper. Wash and dry seven or eight sage leaves. When you are ready to bake, spread the onion rings on top of the *schiacciata*, pressing them lightly into the dough. Arrange the sage leaves here and there on top of the onion and bathe the surface with a generous amount of olive oil. Consign the bread to the oven and cook it as instructed.

Instead of the sage leaves you may like to add a few anchovy fillets, broken up into pieces and pressed into the dough.

Schiacciata con Pomodoro
Hearthbread Seasoned with Tomato

dough
tomato paste
olive oil
rosemary
garlic

Make the *schiacciata* as described in the master recipe (see page 122) but season it with the following mixture before putting it into the hot oven to bake.

Mix a tablespoon of concentrated tomato paste into a tablespoon of olive oil and paint this lightly over the surface of the dough. Then press on to the dough a few sprigs of tender fresh rosemary, one or two crisp garlic cloves shaved into thin slices and a pinch of coarse salt.

When describing the additions that one may use to embellish this basic flat bread to enhance its flavour and interest, one soon begins to perceive how the modern pizza in all its garnished glory came about.

Schiacciata con L'Uva
Hearthbread with Fresh Grapes

grapes
flour
sugar
yeast

This *schiacciata* has a sweet element in it and was made, originally, in the Chianti area of Tuscany by country housewives at the time of the *vendemmia*, the autumn grape harvest. In this season, of course, there are grapes to spare and this fruit-laden bread is a good example of the Tuscan housewives' ingenuity in making a day-to-day food into something festive and seasonal. It was also sometimes confected with withered grapes that were hung to dry from the rafters for many months until they were ready to be made into Vin Santo di Caratello, a delicious dessert wine when made, in the old manner, from air-dried grapes and matured in the barrel. Bread made with vin santo grapes, honey and black pepper is called *panepazzo*.

A similar *schiacciata* is made in Conegliano in the Veneto, another wine area, where it is called *pinza* and is made from bread dough mixed with honey and dried fruit, and is enlivened

with black pepper to provoke a thirst. As raisins and sultanas are available all year round the enjoyment of this bread was not solely confined to the *vendemmia* as was the Tuscan version.

The grapes used in *Schiacciata con L'Uva* are normally either the sweet aleatico or the chianti grape, sangiovese, which produces a sharper flavour. I have successfully used small seedless ruby red grapes with a muscat flavour. Today *Schiacciata con L'Uva* is often served as a dessert but I like it for a special breakfast instead of a brioche or croissant. The following recipe made with a very soft dough will make a pliant bread rather like an English tea cake. It will glisten and crackle with sugar, and the plump grapes in it burst appealingly with liquid flavour.

To make this schiacciata, *which is sufficient for 4 to 6 people, you will need for the dough 14 oz/4 cups/400 g of half plain strong flour or American all-purpose flour and half plain cake flour; 1 oz/a scant ¼ cup/25 g of white sugar; a large pinch of salt; about 8 fl oz/1 cup/225 ml of hand-hot water, depending on the absorbancy of the flour; 1 level teaspoon of dried active yeast granules, plus 1 teaspoon of white sugar. To season the* schiacciata *you will need 12 oz/3½ cups/340 g of small seedless ruby grapes or small red wine grapes; 5 tablespoons of white sugar. Oven temperatures: 225°F/100°C/¼; 400°F/200°C/6.*

Put the flour, sugar and the pinch of salt into a large warm bowl. Mix them together with a fork. With a little of the warm water dissolve the yeast and sugar and let the mixture stand until it creams and fizzes. Pour the working yeast into the flour and mix it in with a fork. Gradually add the rest of the water until you have mixed all the flour into a ball of soft dough. Put the ball on to a lightly floured work surface and knead it until it is smooth but still soft; add a sprinkle of flour occasionally if the dough is sticky but try to keep it soft and springy and on the moist side. Continue kneading for about ten minutes.

Form the dough into a ball and place it in a clean but flour-sprinkled warm bowl. Make a cross with a sharp knife in the top of the dough as this will help it rise. Cover the bowl with a plastic bag and leave it aside in a warm draught-free place. The dough will take anything from thirty minutes to two to three hours to rise depending on the room temperature, and should become more than twice its original size.

Meanwhile, pull the grapes off their stems and wash them, discarding any that are not perfectly sound. Dry them with kitchen paper and put them in a single layer in a flat pottery dish. Put the dish into the oven, preheated to the first temperature, until they are hot and sticky, but not at bursting point, about fifteen minutes. Remove the grapes and turn the oven to the second setting.

Take the risen dough and cut it in half with a sharp knife. Knead the pieces briefly. Lay one piece on a buttered round flat twelve inch pizza pan and press it out with your hands into a ten to eleven inch circle. The dough should be about half an inch thick, and soft and springy. Take a little more than half the hot grapes and press them into the dough with your fingers; when they are all well-embedded sprinkle one tablespoon or so of the sugar all over them.

Take the second ball of dough and on the floured surface spread it out with your palms and fingers into roughly the same shape as the first piece. Lay the dough like a plump quilt on top of the grapes to make a sandwich and press it lightly down and around them and all around the edge, but without any folding and pinching. The idea is to combine the two puffy layers of dough where they touch. Take the rest of the grapes and spread them evenly all over the top of the *schiacciata*, again pressing them gently into the dough.

Cover the bread loosely with a plastic bag and leave it in the warm kitchen for thirty to forty-five minutes to rise for the second time. When it has risen another half inch or so, sprinkle the rest of the sugar with a sifter spoon all over the surface of the dough. Be generous and let the sugar drift in the hollows where the grapes are.

Put the *schiacciata* into the hot oven and let it bake for about thirty minutes, until the top is golden and glistens with the melted sugar. Before you are tempted to eat a piece, let it cool a little as the juicy grapes, hot from the oven, will burn your lips.

Schiacciata con I Ciccioli
Hearthbread with Pork Scrappling

dough
bacon
lard or butter
olive oil
black pepper

Schiacciata con I Ciccioli was a rustic invention using spare bread dough from the weekly baking and a delicious trifle from the family pig to make a savoury treat.

In the rural areas of Tuscany and Umbria, pigs are an important part of the country dweller's economy. During the months of December and January most country houses have a large board propped up outside and suspended from it will be a pig being carefully butchered to produce *prosciutti* and *salami* to last the year round. *Ciccioli* are the small caramelized fragments of protein that appear when pork fat is rendered down for lard, they are crisp and have a good flavour. Outside Italy, they are not likely to be readily available unless you live on a farm and butcher your own pigs. So, to achieve a similar texture, use instead bacon or *pancetta*, chopped and fried until it is crisp.

Italian countrywomen, like their grandmothers and great-grandmothers, take enjoyment in the quality of their daily food and use whatever is at hand to embellish simple dishes. Years ago there was no distinction made between sweet and savoury things and both elements were used together quite freely. In fact, this recipe for *Schiacciata con I Ciccioli* is a simple version of one that contained sugar, eggs, candied fruit, pine kernels and cinnamon – a mixture of tastes that no longer pleases the conventional palate.

To make a good-sized schiacciata *(sufficient for 4 to 6 people) you will need* all *the dough from the master recipe on page 122, but use 1 whole teaspoon of yeast granules instead of* ½ *teaspoon. Then you will need 4 oz/1 cup/100 g of diced raw bacon or pancetta (thick slices of bacon are best to achieve neat square dice); a little olive oil to fry the bacon; a walnut-sized lump of soft lard or butter or 1 tablespoon of olive oil; a good pinch of black pepper. Oven temperature: 425°F/220°C/7.*

Prepare the dough according to the recipe on page 122 up to and including the first rising in a warm draught-free place. Meanwhile fry the diced bacon or pancetta in a very little oil until crisp. When the bacon is golden remove it from the pan and allow it to drain thoroughly on kitchen paper.

When the dough has risen take it from the bowl and knock it back; as you press and knead you will hear the air hissing out. Now flatten the dough and lay on it small pieces of the softened lard or butter or sprinkle on the oil. Fold the dough over and knead it until the fat is amalgamated. You may need an extra spray of flour at this point to dry the surface of the dough. Next sprinkle a large pinch of pepper over the bacon and knead it into the dough; this will take about three to five minutes for the bacon to become well-incorporated.

Have ready a round flat twelve inch pizza pan which must be lightly oiled. Flatten the ball of dough and lay it in the pan; then with your palms and fingers spread it evenly over the pan until it is almost full; the dough should be about half an inch thick. Set it aside in a warm place, the table in a fairly warm 70°F/24°C kitchen is perfect, cover it with a plastic bag or a clean kitchen cloth and let it prove for thirty to forty-five minutes. The dough will rise another half inch or so.

Have the oven heating up to the required temperature, and when it is hot bake the *schiacciata* on a central shelf for twenty minutes. Watch to see that the top does not become too brown, if it is in danger of this cover it with foil.

This *schiacciata* is delicious eaten hot or cold instead of bread; when it is cold the peppery flavour is more intense. I like it split and filled with fresh ripe tomatoes. In Tuscan Cortona a similar bread is baked in tall moulds and sold before Lent.

Pizza Perugina
Pizza in the Perugian Manner

dough
prosciutto
pecorino
parmesan
egg
butter
olive oil

This flat bread enriched with cheese, *prosciutto* and eggs is an Umbrian elaboration on the theme of simple hearthbread. Umbria, one of the two regions in Italy to have no coastline, makes up for the lack of the sight of the sea with numerous rivers, lush green valleys and dense forests; it is the green heart of the peninsula. Although the Umbrians protest that their cuisine is made up of the most simple *piatti poveri*, that is plain dishes eaten by the poor, I have always found that Umbrian dishes have a rich complication of flavour and ingredient that belies their modest pretensions. In fact, it is the Umbrians whom Catullus described as being 'well fed', and who are the ones who slice truffles and scatter them over their *bruschetta*, the ever-popular and simple toasted bread rubbed with a cut clove of garlic then drenched in olive oil and sprinkled with crystalline salt.

This bread will have an appetizing golden crust and a strong fragrance of hot cheese. Inside it will be a soft yellow colour studded with pink *prosciutto*. *Pizza Perugina* is delicious when warm, cut into narrow triangular slices and served as part of an antipasto, with perhaps a dish of aubergines stewed with olive oil, garlic and tomatoes; or fresh young broad beans still in their pods, *salame* and *capocollo*, cured pork.

To make a Pizza Perugina *sufficient for 4 or 5 people you will need all the dough from the master recipe on page 122, but use 1 whole teaspoon of yeast granules instead of ½ teaspoon. Then, to season the pizza you will need 1 oz/1 tablespoon/25 g of butter; 3 oz/1 loosely packed cup/80 g of lean* prosciutto *cut into tiny squares; 2 oz/1 loosely packed cup/50 g of freshly grated pecorino cheese and the same amount of parmesan; a little black pepper; 1 large egg; 1 tablespoon of olive oil; a little butter or lard for greasing. Oven temperatures: 425°F/220°C/7; 350°F/180°C/4.*

First make up the dough according to the method described in the master recipe for *schiacciata* on page 122, up to and including the first rising.

When the dough has doubled in volume put it on to a large, lightly floured work surface and press it out flat; cut the butter into tiny pieces and distribute them over the dough. Fold the dough over and knead it; repeat this folding two or three times to incorporate the butter, then knead in the small squares of *prosciutto*, the grated cheeses and the black pepper. Add the egg; at this point the dough will be sticky and

Pizza Quattro Stagione in Naples

Women selling wild mushrooms at Palazzo del Pero

messy, so use a very little extra flour to help you quench the egg. Lastly add the tablespoon of olive oil and a little more flour if needed. Knead the dough firmly for a few minutes to make sure the ingredients are well and evenly dispersed.

Have ready a twelve inch flat pizza tin greased with butter or lard. Take the ball of dough and put it into the middle of the tin, then with your palms and fingers flatten and spread the dough out evenly to almost fill the space; the dough should be about one inch thick, and dimpled. Cover the bread loosely with a plastic bag and leave it in a warm draught-free corner of the kitchen to rise for the second time. This will take forty-five minutes to an hour and the bread will grow a little more.

Have the oven heating to the first temperature. When the dough is sufficiently risen prick it here and there with a fork and bake it on a middle shelf for twenty-five to thirty minutes; the first fifteen minutes at the high temperature and the last ten to fifteen minutes at the lower temperature.

To vary the texture of this bread it is a pleasant idea to dice the pecorino cheese instead of grating it and to reserve a little of the tiny dice to press into the top of the dough before it goes into the oven. In this way the scraps of cheese will melt into caramel-coloured beads and will smell delicious. You may also use a lump of *prosciutto* cut into dice instead of thin slices cut into squares, and this too will give a good texture to the bread.

Schiacciata con Cipolle ed Ulive
Rustic Pie filled with Onion and Olives

This dish although called a *schiacciata* borders on the realms of a country pie as it is made up of a filling and two separate sheets of dough. The filling contains the sort of ingredients that would be easily available to an Italian *massaia*, the matriarch: preserved olives from the groves, capers home-pickled from the caper plants growing on old stone walls, an onion or two from the *orto*, vegetable garden, and a few herbs.

dough
onions
black olives
anchovies
capers
parsley
olive oil

To make this savoury bread or pie, which is sufficient for 4-5 people, you will need all the dough produced from the master recipe on page 122, but use half strong flour or American all-purpose flour and half plain cake flour. This will make a softer crust. In Italy I use a 00 flour instead of the 0 grade (see page 22 for a full description and explanation of the differing virtues of flours).

For the filling you will need 2 medium-size strong and spicy onions; 1 tablespoon of olive oil; 2 dozen pitted black olives (remove the pits either by rubbing them through your fingers if the olives are soft or carving the flesh off with a knife if they are hard); 2 tablespoons of well-drained capers preserved in wine vinegar (if they are preserved in any other type of vinegar rinse them before using); 3 anchovy fillets; 3 sprigs of parsley; salt and freshly milled black pepper; 3 more tablespoons of olive oil for garnishing the crust. Oven temperatures: 450°F/240°C/8; 400°F/200°C/6.

First make the dough according to the instructions on page 122, up to and including the first rising.

Slice the onions into fine rings and soften them in the olive oil over a medium heat until they are a pale golden colour. Leave them aside to cool. On a large chopping block pile the pitted olives, capers, anchovy fillets and parsley. With a *mezzaluna* or sharp knife chop all these together until you have a 'trittata', a pile of evenly chopped ingredients; however do not chop them so fine as to make a paste but leave them with a nice judged texture. Next, combine the onion with the *trittata*, mixing all together with a fork and seasoning with an abundance of black pepper and a little salt.

Meanwhile the oven has been heating to the first temperature setting and the dough has risen.

Knock back the dough and knead it again for three to five minutes. Divide it into two parts, one slightly larger than the other. Roll out the larger piece and with it cover an oiled twelve inch round flat pizza tin. Roll out the second smaller portion and let it rest for ten minutes on a lightly floured surface. When the dough has rested spread the filling over the dough in the tin taking it evenly almost up to the edges. Next lay the smaller disc on top of the filling. Fold the lower edge of the dough up and over the top; fold and pinch as you work your way around the pie to make a good seal.

Next prick the surface here and there with a fork and paint on two tablespoons of olive oil.

Put the *schiacciata* into the hot oven on the central shelf and bake for ten minutes; then reduce the heat to the second setting and bake for another ten minutes or until the crust is golden. As soon as the pie is done take it from the oven and paint on the remaining tablespoon of olive oil, which will give the crust a momentary shine and will craze the surface like the glaze on a Titian.

This savoury *schiacciata* is excellent served hot or cold with a light red wine.

Torta Condita Umbra
Seasoned Soda Bread

This is an easily and quickly made savoury bread to be eaten warm, and is prepared without baker's yeast. Originally the Umbrian housewife would have used just a pinch of bicarbonate of soda and then would have baked the dough on the *testo* or *pannaio* over the open fire; the bread would have been dense and heavy and, perforce, eaten warm. Today, in Italy, small packets of baking powder are especially got up for savoury doughs – unlike raising agents for cakes and pastries these are not mixed with vanilla-flavoured flours.

flour
parmesan
eggs
butter
milk
baking soda

The manner of making soda bread, however, is quite different from that of yeast-leavened bread. A yeast dough is handled robustly and left to its own devices to rise over long periods of time. With soda bread, as soon as the liquid part of the recipe comes into contact with the baking soda the chemical raising starts with the formation of carbonic acid gas, and the dough must be quickly and lightly handled and put into the oven immediately to receive the benefit of the aeration.

To make a small Torta Condita *you will need 10½ oz/3 cups/300 g of plain or all-purpose flour; 2 oz/¾ cup/50 g of freshly grated parmesan cheese; 1 teaspoon of salt; black pepper; 1 teaspoon of baking powder; 2 oz/½ stick/50 g of butter; 6 tablespoons of milk; 2 medium-sized eggs. Oven temperature: 375°F/190°C/5.*

Have the oven heating to the correct temperature. Combine all the dry ingredients in a large mixing bowl and sift them well together with a fork, paying particular attention to the baking powder, as it must be well-mixed through the flour.

In a small saucepan melt the butter over a low heat, then off the heat add the milk and the eggs, whisking the liquid until it is thoroughly mixed.

Next pour the liquid into the dry ingredients and mix them together with a fork; when the dough comes together knead it very briefly and lightly, adding a sprinkling of flour or a little more milk if need be. The dough should be soft. Pick up the ball of dough, place it on a buttered flat pizza tin or oven sheet and push it with your palms into a rough circle about nine inches in diameter and half an inch thick. Put the *torta* straight into the preheated oven – it will take twenty minutes to bake.

The crust should be a good golden brown and have a pleasant crisp texture, the bread itself will be yellow from the eggs and have an agreeable scent from the parmesan.

Focaccia con Le Olive Verde
Hearthbread with Green Olives

dough
green olives

Focaccia is the Ligurian name for *schiacciata*. Along the Ponentine coast rich olive groves provide the justly famous Ligurian olive oil, which is lighter and more akin to French oils than to the Tuscan kind. Olives too are preserved here, and they find their way into the delicious *focacce di olive* of Genoa, bread dough sown with black olives and then liberally irrigated with cold olive oil after the bread is baked. The result is delicious; rich, salty and very oily. This recipe is lighter and crisper and makes a pleasant table bread for those who like green olives.

To make this focaccia *you will need* all *the dough as given on page 122. To garnish the* focaccia *you will need about 15 pitted green olives; a little cold water and a pastry brush with which to apply it; a sprinkling of coarse salt. Oven temperature: 425°F/220°C/7.*

Prepare the dough according to the recipe on page 122 up to and including the first rising, and have ready a twelve inch round flat pizza tin oiled with olive oil. When the dough is risen knead it again briefly, then take the ball of dough and with your palms and fingers spread it out on the tin until it almost fills the space; it should be about half an inch thick, and unevenly dimpled.

Take the olives and press them into the dough here and there over its surface. Cover the *focaccia* loosely with a clean kitchen cloth and leave it to rise for the second time in a warm draught-free corner of the kitchen. This will take about forty-five minutes and the dough will swell half an inch or more.

Have the oven heating to the correct temperature. Paint some cold water over the surface of the dough, pushing the olives further into its depths if need be. The water will give a crisp crackling crust. Sprinkle on a little salt and bake the *focaccia* for about twenty minutes on a central shelf of the oven.

Foccacia con Le Olive Nere *Hearthbread with Black Olives*

dough
black dried
olives
olive oil

This is very typical of Genoa. To make it, simply break about ten *olive toste*, dried olives, into pieces, discard the pits and knead the fragments lightly into the dough after the first rising before you shape the *focaccia* as above. Let it rise a second time and bake it as instructed but do not paint on the cold water. When the *focaccia* is baked, sprinkle on the salt and a great deal of good olive oil.

Focaccia con Il Formaggio
Hearthbread with Cheese

This *focaccia* has a lovely scent of cheese; contrast its bready texture with the more cake-like *Torta Condita Umbra*, the cheese-flavoured soda-risen bread given on page 131.

dough
parmesan or pecorino

To make this focaccia *you will need all the dough as given on page 122. To season it you will need 2 oz/1 loosely packed cup/50 g of freshly grated parmesan or pecorino cheese – parmesan will give a sweeter more mellow flavour whilst pecorino is sharper and more savoury; a good sprinkle of freshly milled black pepper; a little cold water. Oven temperature: 425°F/220°C/7.*

Prepare the dough according to the recipe on page 122 up to and including the first rising. Have ready an eleven to twelve inch round flat pizza tin oiled with olive oil. When the dough is ready, knead it for the second time on a lightly floured surface, and as you knead add the grated cheese into which you have sprinkled the black pepper. Make sure that the cheese is evenly spread through the dough.

Press the dough into the tin until it nearly fills the circle and is about three quarters of an inch thick. Cover it lightly and leave it aside in a warm part of the kitchen to rise for about forty-five minutes. Heat the oven. Just before you put the *focaccia* into the hot oven pierce the surface here and there with the tines of a fork and paint on a little cold water. The *focaccia* will take twenty minutes to bake on the central shelf of the oven.

Focaccia con Vino Bianco e Salvia
Hearthbread with White Wine and Sage

This bread is lovely eaten warm when the scent is green and winy. Do not be tempted to put more than just a little wine into the dough as a flavouring; if you substitute wine for the water for mixing the dough the bread will be hard and heavy.

dough
sage leaves
dry white wine

To make this scented focaccia *you will need all the dough as given on page 122. To garnish the* focaccia *you will need 15 to 20 tender fresh sage leaves; a little ground black pepper; 1 tablespoon of dry white wine; a little cold water. Oven temperature: 425°F/220°C/7.*

Prepare the dough according to the recipe on page 122 up to and including the first rising, and have ready a twelve inch round flat pizza tin oiled with olive oil. Cut the sage leaves into tiny shreds with a *mez-*

zaluna or sharp knife and sprinkle them with black pepper – by sprinkling the leaves with the pepper you make it easier for the pepper to penetrate the dough evenly, carried there by the larger particles.

When the dough is risen take it from the bowl and knead it briefly on a floured board, adding the sage leaves a little at a time and sprinkling on the white wine; knead the dough until all the extra ingredients are well-mixed in, using a little more flour if necessary, but be careful not to overwork it.

Flatten the dough with your hands and press it into the tin in a rough circle a little smaller than the tin. Leave the *focaccia*, lightly covered, to rise again in a warm draught-free corner of the room. After about forty-five minutes paint the surface of the dough with a light coat of water, pierce the *focaccia* in parallel lines with the tines of a fork and consign it to the middle shelf of the oven which must be at the correct temperature. The *focaccia* will take about twenty minutes to bake.

LA PIADINA
BAKESTONE BREAD

Piadina is amongst the simplest and oldest of hearthbreads. It comes from the Romagna, a northerly region of Italy which stretches from the eastern coast right up to the city of Bologna. Through its fertile plain runs the ancient Roman Via Emilia which leads from Rimini on the Adriatic to Piacenza on the edges of Lombardy.

Romagna is always coupled, sometimes to its chagrin, with Emilia. Recently there has been a movement to declare Romagna an administrative region in its own right, severing its links with Emilia. In a recent discussion on the subject local politicians and poets heatedly debated the merits, defects and complications of the scheme. Which of the region's large towns should become first in importance: Ravenna, Forlì, Cesena or Rimini? What was to be done with the thirty-two separate folk museums, a strong symptom of the region's natural divisiveness? What was *not* under discussion was the *piadine* being cooked for the debaters by a smiling Romagnoli woman. Neither was there any argument about the full red Sangiovese wine that fuelled their debate. Food and drink remain one of the strongest manifestations of culture.

One summer day while visiting Ravenna, the glittering Byzantine city of Romagna, we had to wait outside the gates of St. Apollinare in Classe as the Basilica was at that moment closed on account of a private service.

Suddenly the massive main doors were opened, and to the sound of organ and trumpet a wedding procession moved triumphantly through the long nave towards daylight. The church became flooded with sight-seers, guests and clergy; talking, parading and admiring the handsome bridal couple and their attendants. Towering above, the cool green-blue mosaics floated aloof; the white sheep, symbolizing the twelve Apostles, spaced around the rood arch in their own static procession from Jerusalem and Bethlehem towards Christ.

The wedding reception was being held at the neighbouring rest-aurant and being busy the proprietor could not provide us with lunch. However he did offer us local *Romagnolo* wine and *piadine*. I was expecting something quite ordinary and possible factory-made, but when the *piadine* arrived they were newly baked, supple gold discs of soft bread folded around slices of salty *prosciutto* and melting gorgon-zola, unusually soft and hot from the bakestone.

La Piadina was the unleavened country bread of the poor Romag-noli, made simply from kneaded flour, salt and water, flattened into thin cakes and baked on hot stones or clay *testi*, which were heated over fires made from whatever sticks could be collected. When the *piadine* were cooked the circles were cut with a knife into four quarters, called in Romagnoli dialect *quadrett*. Ancient Roman bread when similarly cut was called *quadrae*. The *contadini* ate this simple but appetizing unlea-vened bread with wild salads, and perhaps some cheese or a little saus-age if times were good.

Poets have written long poems about the humble *piadina*, and now, as a symbol of the region's past, it is eaten all over Romagna in simple bars and chic restaurants, and plays a prominent part at local festas.

Piadine are extremely easy to cook, delicious to eat and look impres-sive on the table. As the dough contains no yeast, like the unleavened bread of the Bible, it does not take up any time for rising, neither is it cooked in the oven. The dough is simply mixed, left for twenty minutes or so for the gluten to develop and then cooked on a hot bakestone. If you do not have one, an un-oiled heavy frying pan makes a perfectly adequate alternative. The breads take just a few minutes to cook and are excellent split to make hot sandwiches or left entire as the base for an open sandwich. The only problem that may arise is that you might find you are unable to cook them fast enough to keep up with the eaters; they tend to disappear directly they leave the pan.

The old recipe for *piadine* uses just flour and water and maybe a little lard, but there are more modern versions which include olive oil, milk and a trace of baking powder, which help to make the *piadine* softer.

Piadina
Bakestone Bread

flour
baking soda
olive oil
milk

To make a piadina *sufficient for 4 people you will need 10½ oz/3 cups/ 300 g of strong or American all-purpose flour; 1 teaspoon of salt; ½ teaspoon of baking powder; 3 tablespoons of olive oil; ¼ pint/a generous ½ cup/150 ml of a mixture of half milk, half water.*

Mix the flour, salt and baking powder in a large bowl. Make a well in the centre and pour in the olive oil and a little of the milk/water mixture. Start to mix the dough with a fork, gradually adding the rest of the liquid; you may need a little extra water, depending on the absorbancy of the flour. When the dough has come together and leaves the sides of the bowl clean, form it into a rough ball and put it on a very lightly floured surface. Knead the dough until it is smooth, which will take about ten minutes. Let the dough rest for ten to thirty minutes, at your convenience.

When the dough has rested divide it into small balls each about the size of a plum. Roll each ball out into a flat circle about an eighth of an inch thick. Now put the heavy frying pan or bakestone on to a medium heat. Let the pan become hot enough to make a drop of water dance.

Put the first *piadina* into the pan and press it down with a wooden spatula. Let it cook on one side for twenty seconds or so; when you lift it to turn it over it should have whitened and there will be the faint beginnings of small brown scorch marks. Repeat this with the second side of the *piadina* and turn the bread two or three times during the cooking. When the bread is ready it should have small brown spots over its surface; as soon as you have achieved this effect put the cooked *piadina* on a wire cake rack and proceed with the next one.

Serve them hot, with slices of *prosciutto, salame* or cheese, and perhaps olives, radishes or a little tomato for a quick lunch; not forgetting, of course, some cheerful red country wine.

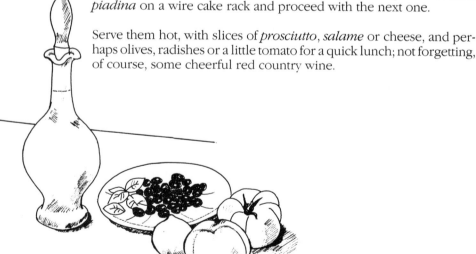

TORTA DI GRANOTURCO
MAIZE FLOUR BREAD

As well as providing variety by adding diverse flavours to a basic *schiacciata*, country housewives would also make *torte*, cakes, or *pizze* as they are sometimes called, out of different types of flours, which produce different flavours and textures. Amongst these is the yellow maize or Indian corn flour called *farina di granoturco*, which is more usually employed in the making of *polenta*. During the last century many peasant families lived on a diet of bread made solely from this *granoturco*, and this resulted in vitamin deficiencies which caused the people to suffer from pellagra. Other flours used were *farina di ceci*, chick-pea flour, which makes the truly delicious *Farinata*, and *farina di castagna*, which goes into rustic desserts and cakes like *Castagnaccia* and *Baldino di Castagna*. Rustic *focacce* are also made with potatoes.

Torta di Granoturco was originally made on the hot *schiacce*, flat hearthstones, and is simply and quickly made without the aid of leavening. It was difficult to turn the paste-like dough over to crisp both sides of the cake, so very often a metal lid or a cover of thick paper covered with ashes was used to bake the top to a crackling gold. The *torta* was served hot with *verdura rifatta*, dark-leaved greens like spinach, beet greens or chard; boiled then squeezed dry of all moisture, cut into ribbons and finished in a shallow pan with olive oil and garlic, sometimes a little *peperoncino*. And very handsome the golden sun-coloured wheel of maize cake looks too when served with the dark green mass. The ever economical peasant women would serve any *avanze*, uneaten scraps, of the bread crumbled into the *verdura* and heated through with more oil and garlic.

Torta di Granoturco
Maize Flour Bread

When this *torta* is baked it will be a deep golden colour and have the crisp chewy texture of a biscuit.

polenta flour
plain flour
olive oil

To make a Torta di Granoturco *you will need 7 oz/1½ cups/200 g of coarse ground polenta flour, that is maize or Indian corn flour; 4 oz/1 cup/100 g of plain cake or all-purpose flour; ½ teaspoon of salt*

*and a large pinch of freshly ground black pepper; 2 tablespoons of
olive oil; 7 fl oz/1 scant cup/ 200 ml of hot water; another tablespoon
of olive oil to spread over the surface of the cake. Oven temperature:
400°F/200°C/6.*

Tip the yellow and white flours into a bowl with the salt and pepper.
Blend them well with the aid of a fork so that you are left with a heap of
pale yellow grains. Next pour two tablespoons of olive oil into the hot
water (this will help the oil spread evenly through the flour), tip the
liquid into the flour and mix well with a fork until you have a soft paste
with the grainy texture of marzipan.

Meanwhile have your oven heating to the required temperature.
Lightly grease with butter a round twelve inch pizza tin. Take the lump
of paste and place it in the centre of the tin, then with the palms of your
hands and your fingers spread the mass until it covers the whole surface of the tin. It should be little more than half an inch thick when you
have finished.

Prick the surface here and there with the tines of a fork, sprinkle on
a tablespoon of olive oil and put the *torta* into the hot oven on a
middle shelf where it will take about twenty minutes to cook.

Serve the *torta* hot either with the traditional green-leaved vegetables
described above re-cooked in a pan or with a tomato salad flavoured
with basil, olive oil and *aceto balsamico*. *Aceto balsamico* is a flavoursome wine vinegar which is aged and kept in oak barrels for many
years before it is sold in pretty and costly glass bottles. It is a speciality
of Modena and well worth the expense. Home-made *aceto balsamico*
is prized above rubies.

FARINATA
CHICK-PEA FLOUR BREAD

There are references to *'pan di Ceci'* as far back as the 14th century and it seems that *Farinata* is native to Genoa and the Ligurian coast. It also travelled as far as Florence, perhaps carried there by the mercantile trade from Pisa along the river Arno; in Florence it is sometimes called *Cecina*. There is a *Genovese* legend about the birth of *Farinata*, a somewhat unlikely tale but amusing. On August 6th 1284 the bloody and terrible sea battle of Meloria took place between the Pisans and the Genoese, the culmination of years of rivalry for supremacy over sea passages and lucrative trade. The Pisans in their 72 brave galleons lost, and the Genoese, who had 88 barques, triumphantly took 9,000 prisoners back with them to Genoa. And so was born the saying *'Chi vuol veder Pisa vada a Genova'* – 'If you want to see Pisa go to Genoa'.

The prisoners were transported by ship and it was on one of these vessels that *Farinata* was invented. In those days chick-peas were used on long voyages as a durable food stuff and this prison ship had the accustomed sacks of dried peas on board, stored next to several barrels of oil. During the journey they were assailed by a fierce storm and the ship was besieged and buffeted by the waves for many days. The sacks of peas were in the hold and of course became soaked and tossed around in the salt water; the oil barrels burst and added to the confusion. When the storm died down the Genoese found that the hold was awash with a soup of chick-peas; famous for their parsimony, they gave this mess to the Pisan prisoners to eat. Some Pisans refused the fare and left it on their plates. During the hot sun of the day the mess dried into cakes, which interested the Genoese who then decided to try it out in their ovens. Thus did *Oro di Pisa*, Pisan gold, come about.

I first tasted *Farinata* in the small seaside town of Varazze which lies between Genoa and Savona. I was in fact searching for *Sardenaira*, the much written-of Ligurian Pizza (see page 70) of which, it appeared, the Varazze bakers had not heard. Perhaps I should have recalled that one finds Pisa in Genoa and gone elsewhere.

Varazze, where Rose Macauley the novelist and travel writer spent many years of her childhood, is a modest town with, for its population, an inordinate amount of *pasticcerie* and bakers' shops. They specialize in delicious biscuits called *Baci di Nonna*, Grandmother's Kisses, bitter-sweet almond macaroons and *Farinata*.

Chick-pea flour is not particularly easy to find even in Italy. Regional cooking is so particular to its zone that grocers will not stock an unusual ingredient if the local cuisine does not call for it. So, outside the Ligurian coast and some northern areas chick-pea flour is generally only to be found in specialist shops. It is sometimes available in health food shops in Britain and the United States, and I give a recipe for chick-pea flour bread (*Farinata*) as it is flavourful and interesting.

Farinata
Chick-Pea Flour Bread

chick-pea flour
olive oil

To make enough Farinata *to fill a twelve inch round flat tin that is half an inch deep you will need 8 oz/2 cups/240 g of* farina di ceci, *chick-pea flour; 14 fl oz/slightly less than 2 cups/400 ml of cold water; 1 heaped teaspoon of salt; 6 tablespoons of olive oil; abundant black pepper. Oven temperature: 425°F/220°C/7.*

In a medium-sized bowl mix the chick-pea flour with the cold water, do this with a little liquid at a time so that you will avoid lumps. The consistency should be of a thin batter which just coats the back of a metal spoon. Leave the mixture for several hours, even overnight if it is more convenient, so that the flour is completely slaked. When you are ready to bake, skim off the slight froth that will have formed on the surface of the bowl, and remove a spoon or so of water if there is a great deal on top of the batter. Stir the mixture again well with a fork and add the salt.

PIZZE CALDE
FARINATA

Have the oven heating to the required temperature. Pour the olive oil into the flat tin then on top pour in the batter; the oil will float up and over the edges of the batter. With a fork gently mix the oil and the batter together until they are as well amalgamated as possible. You can mix the olive oil into the batter before putting it into the tin, and in this case you will need extra olive oil to oil the tin. I prefer to use the first, traditional, method because of its oddity.

Put the *Farinata* into the hot oven and let it bake until the top is a deep rich gold, about thirty minutes. To serve it, preferably slightly warm, grind on a great deal of black pepper and cut it into slices.

Farinata, which should never be more than half an inch thick, should be well saturated in the oil and have a dense and heavy texture when cut into; the flour is extremely light and powdery and very absorbent and needs the long period of soaking in water to slake it completely. If this is not completely accomplished the *Farinata* can be powdery and unpleasant. There are other methods of preparing *Farinata* which involve boiling it in water, rather like polenta, for an hour before baking it. However as you have to stir the mixture continuously to prevent it sticking I think the soaking method is preferable.

In Liguria they often embellish *Farinata* with thinly sliced raw onion or thinly sliced young artichokes. If you wish to do this it is better to cook the *Farinata* for five to ten minutes first to drive off some of the liquid, and then scatter the onions or artichoke evenly over the surface, as when the *Farinata* is put in the oven it is very watery and the garnish will sink to the bottom of the pan. You may also garnish it with a few sprigs of rosemary if you are partial to that flavour.

Farinata or *Cecina* is absolutely delicious, it makes a good addition to a varied antipaste or can be simply served with white wine.

FOCACCIA DI PATATE
POTATO TART

Apulia is the region that forms the high heel of Italy's shoe and the clock on her stocking. In antiquity it was Greek, part of *Magna Graecia*, and the near 1,000 years of Hellenic civilisation is stamped deeply in the culture and the customs of the Pugliese. They grow the glorious Mediterranean crops of wheat, olives and wine. There is fruit in abundance, vegetables, especially potatoes, and shoals of fish and shellfish from the sea. Their bread, of which they eat a great deal, comes in large loaves made from robust unrefined flour and is leavened with sourdough yeast, kept going, some say, for hundreds of years. Like the ancient Greeks and Romans their generous second breakfast, *merenda*, consists of bread with a relish, a *frisa*, which is a wholewheat small round bread split and soaked with olive oil then stuffed with raw onion and ripe tomato, eaten with a glass of wine; *frisa* is not so unlike the Niçoise *pan bagnat*.

The Pugliese grow and enjoy potatoes, which play a more interesting part in the region's cooking than in any other area of Italy. *Tiella*, a cousin of *paella*, is a delicious legacy from the Spanish occupation of Bari, but substitutes potato for rice. The secondary ingredients can alter to suit the taste of the cook but the potatoes must remain; cooked in an earthenware dish and covered, perhaps, by layers of parsley mixed with spicy onions and a strata of mussels sprinkled with grated cheese and coarse breadcrumbs, irrigated with olive oil. Taranto has a potato dish too, called a *Torta di Taranto*, made from tomatoes and mozzarella laid on a bed of creamed potatoes and seasoned with the indispensable olive oil, oregano and black pepper. In fact, a potato pizza. Similarly, this *focaccia* is really a potato tart.

Focaccia di Patate alla Pugliese
Potato Tart in the Apulian Manner

potatoes
prosciutto
parmesan
eggs
dry white wine

To make this focaccia *you will need 1 lb/350 g of potatoes; 2 oz/1 cup/50 g of* prosciutto *cut into small pieces, or 4 oz/2 cups/100 g raw* pancetta *or bacon, diced and fried; 2 oz/1 cup/50 g of freshly grated* parmesan cheese; salt and black pepper; 2 whole eggs plus 1 egg yolk; 3½ fl oz/⅓ cup/100 ml of dry white wine. Oven temperature: 350°F/180°C/4.*

Wash and peel the potatoes and grate them through the large holes on a cheese grater. Put the potatoes as you grate them into a bowl of cold water. When they are all grated, rinse them well under running water to remove the excess starch and pat them dry with a clean cloth or kitchen paper. In a large bowl mix the potato with the *prosciutto* (or fried *pancetta* or bacon), add the cheese and season with salt and pepper. Beat the eggs together with the white wine and add this liquid to the potatoes, mixing it in well.

Butter a shallow round earthenware dish ten inches in diameter and one inch deep. Tip into it the mixture; it should fill the dish and come level to its top. Put the *Focaccia* into the preheated oven and cook until the potato is tender and the surface crisp and golden. This will take about one hour.

This *Focaccia di Patate alla Pugliese*, served very hot, makes a delicious supper dish and to refresh its rich savoury taste needs only a green salad, perhaps made with the addition of some peppery rocket (arugula) and a lemon juice and olive oil dressing.

SAVOURY
PIES

GENOVA E TORTE GENOVESE
GENOA AND GENOESE PIES

Torte are refined tarts made from fine pastry, as opposed to the robust dough of the pizza, and are filled with all manner of delicate ingredients, usually cooked in some way before being placed in the pastry shell. They played a prominent role on the lavish tables of the wealthy in mediaeval and Renaissance Italy.

> Above all, no banquet was complete without a *torta* – the 'grete pie' of English medieval cooking – a dish which ingeniously evaded the sumptuary law against the serving of more than three courses, by putting both meats and sweets in the same dish. One of these *torte* – whose recipe is given in the *Libro della cucina del secolo XIV* – contained pork, chickens, ham, sausages, onions, parsley, dates, almonds, flour, cheese, eggs, sugar, salt, saffron, and several other spices. First the chickens were fried in oil, then the ham was made into *ravioli*, and then the chickens, sausages, and *ravioli* were laid on layers of pastry, alternating with layers of dates and almonds. The pie was then covered with pastry, and cooked in hot embers. And there is also, in the same book, a fascinating recipe for 'a pie with live birds' – in which live songbirds were put into a pie of which the roof had little windows – the whole pie being then hung on a tree of pastry. 'Wasn't that a dainty dish to set before a king?'.
>
> Iris Origo
> *The Merchant of Prato*

Today *torte* are still relished in Italy but the old courtly recipes have become streamlined, simple but still retaining savour. Genoa is an excellent city in which to hunt for *torta* and *focaccia* prepared in the city's particular style. Its history as one of the old world's most vigorous seaports, its citizens renowned for their trading abilities and adventurous spirit, has had a great effect on its traditional cuisine. Fair Genoa, described by Gustave Flaubert as 'a city all made of marble, with gardens full of roses. A heart-rending beauty', is wedged between the deep Ligurian Sea and the mountains. Now the rose city is hedged by the briers of the *autostrada*. Due to its position there is little shallow water fishing and sparse farming, but with Genoese taste and thrift whatever produce there was and is, they treated and still treat with sensitivity and imagination, sparing neither time nor trouble. Seafarers from this ancient trading city (the first mention of the Mediaeval Guild of Port and Dock Keepers was in 1281) returned from their arduous voyages to India and the Spice Islands in ships laden with heavy-scented pepper, cinnamon and cloves; the mariners, tired of dry *galettes*, chick-peas and

Market stall in Genoa's Vicolo del Amore Perfetto

Focaccia and Torta di Granoturco on an antique plate

the cloying scent of spices, were eager to taste the fresh cool herbs of their native hillsides and soft, new bread.

Today the Genoese are proud of this heritage and proud of the clever way in which they still use the pungent scents of fresh herbs to enliven and perfume their food. This skill was shown to me in the 'Ristorante Le Fate' in Genoa's Via Ruspole. The chef, Angelo Guerra, had prepared a fish *brodo* in which drifted fragments of *branzino*, sea bass. In the *brodo* too, was a large *raviolo*, the delicate envelope sealing in pieces of *orata*, gilt-head bream, and leaves of fresh marjoram, *persa* in Genoese dialect and also in 19th-century Italian. Once bitten into their green taste was almost shocking in intensity but made a perfectly balanced contrast to the smooth *fumet* and was a precise lesson in using a herb to its greatest advantage. In the restaurant's ovens they bake their speciality, small breads shaped like plump fishes. These are often seasoned in the Genoese tradition with shallots, *polpa di oliva*, the crushed pulp of delicate Ligurian olives, and in the winter, lobster. If Naples is the home of *pizza alla Napoletana* then Genoa bred *focaccia*, herb-scented breads and, by way of their sorties into Oriental lands, rich fine-leaved pastry tarts.

The Genoese bakers' shops are a complete delight with the variety of shapes and flavours they create each day. There are troughs of *grissini*, bread sticks, the length of your forearm, some knobbly with scraps of *salame*, some flecked green with sage leaves. There are *pannini* of all sizes; large loaves, triangular in shape and dark in colour, and of course *focacce*, small flat and round or cooked in large oblong trays, some seasoned with broken olives and bathed in their oil after they have been baked, others garnished with dull red tomato, onions and salt. Still others thirst-makingly studded with anchovies; some, on the other hand, quite plain. And then on the shop counters, reposing on wooden platters will be large wheels of cheese-filled *torte*. The best examples of these are to be found in Recco a few miles from Genoa along the coast; here the pastry is fine and thin, the *quagliata*, the curd cheese, liquid and melting, and the edge of the fine flat wheel twisted like the folds in a Saracen's turban.

In the centre of old Genoa, in the Piazza Soziglia, you can enjoy a light luncheon of *Torta Genovese*. These are small round tarts served hot, constructed again from delicate filo-like pastry and filled with a soft bêchamel in which cooked *bietola*, beet greens, have been mixed, all lightly seasoned with nutmeg. Other *torte* are filled with layers of melted strachino, savoury with its lactic tang.

Throughout the city's 16th-century streets lined with sumptuous palaces, down into the warren of mediaeval lanes and alleys behind the old port; everywhere there is a foot of window-sill there will be a pot of green basil, grown from fresh (and freshness is vital) seed. Basil to crush in marble morters, to mix with sharp young pecorino and mellow *parmigiano*, smooth Ligurian olive oil and pine kernels to make Genoa's finest invention, *pesto*. Through the narrow canyon-like alleys one occasionally emerges into a small square filled with a wooden barrow or two holding a discreet display of vegetables. Small in number but perfect in the brilliance of their colours and the soundness of their glossy flesh. Pale lilac aubergines next to scarlet peppers and a froth of emerald flat-leaved parsley. Leaning from the windows of the *vicolo del amore perfetto*, the lane of perfect love, and standing on the grey stone street dressed in flashing gold sequins are sailors' tarts, discussing, of course, what they are going to eat for lunch, some nice slices of Parma ham perhaps and a little parmesan.

Under the arcaded pavements of the *molo* are other market stalls heaped with more vegetables of stunning quality, large piles of *porcini*, fruit, strings of garlic and boxes of olives. In the tiny shops fresh fish is displayed in neat order, gun-metal blue next to the coral of plump red mullet, and round glass jars in which fresh sardines are pressed with large grey and white striped pebbles taken from the shore.

On this street is one of the city's many *friggitorie*, a particular Genoese tradition. These fried food shops open from eleven to one o'clock and from six to eight p.m. and in their wood-fired ovens they bake *farinata* (for recipe see page 140). This, another of their clever inventions, the Genoese, perched at marble-topped tables, eat as a rich snack with a glass of white wine and a piece of bread. The *friggitorie* also sell vegetable fritters, *friscêu*, fried salt cod, *baccala*, and *paniccia*, morsels of fried chick-pea paste. The harbour *friggitoria* which is open to the street has white *tessera* walls on which the word 'Farinata' is picked out in tiny red tile squares. On late summer days they have small round peppers fried to a livid green next to the usual deep dish of *Torta Pasqualina*, one of the triumphs of Genoese cooking (see page 148 for recipe).

The famous Genoese dishes are complicated and need patience to prepare, perhaps the patience of the sailor's wife waiting for the safe return of her husband from the sea. Traditional meat dishes are rare and were reserved for special occasions. *Cima* is one of them and it too needs lengthy preparation. It is made from breast of veal stuffed with sweetbreads and brains, eggs, green vegetables and herbs, all cooked in broth then pressed under weights and served in slices to reveal the pretty mosaic of its interior.

Cappon Magro is another elaborate dish demanding time and the freshest of fish, oysters and vegetables. It is an exceedingly complicated *salade composée*, based on soaked hard biscuits, reminders of the hard tack of the mariners, on which are arranged multicoloured layers of fish and vegetables all cloaked in a *salsa verde* made of anchovies, parsley, capers, pine kernels, oil and vinegar. The whole arrangement is then topped with a large lobster; festal food par excellence!

This notion of intricate festal food brings us back to the *Torta Pasqualina* made especially for Easter, the Queen of all Italian savoury pies. Today, one can eat this *Genovese* delicacy all the year round at many of the city's excellent restaurants and *friggitore*. The classic recipe for it is complicated; the pie requires a great quantity of sheets of paper-thin pastry made from fine white flour, water, salt and Ligurian olive oil. At least fifteen of these almost transparent layers are used to line a deep round dish which is then filled with marjoram-scented spinach, soft *prescinsèua*, a local curd cheese, and raw fresh eggs. The pie is covered with another fifteen layers of pastry veils and pierced here and there with a bodkin to prevent the pastry bursting in the heat of the oven. Although Italian recipe writers remind cooks that they must be careful where they prick the pie so as not to break the egg yolks, they do not give much advice about the size of the dish required, the heat of the oven or the length of cooking time. This sort of information they can safely assume is common knowledge amongst their readers. In Italy the majority of women enjoy a very different culinary heritage to that held by their counterparts in Britain and the United States. Cooking methods and recipes are handed down through the generations, both classic and regional recipes are deeply held manifestations of a powerful culture.

Good pastry cooks are not new in Genoa; in the late 1700s the Genoese palace cook Pietro Santi Puppo wrote a treatise on modern cookery. His preface is worth quoting as in it he lays down a few fundamental rules which still hold good today.

> The principles of good cookery consist firstly in great cleanliness, which will serve the cook by resulting in dishes of good taste and pleasantness to all he has the honour of serving. To pay great attention to the choice of ingredients of whatever type that he has occasion to use, so that they are of the best quality of their kind without any disagreeable odours. For without using good produce one cannot honour or give satisfaction to those one must please, but only bring harm and shame.

> *Il Cuciniere Moderno*

Santi Puppo gives many dainty recipes for pie fillings for feast and fast days (meat and meatless days), clear recipes for both flaky and short-crust pastries, delicious savoury meat dishes and delicate chilled sorbets. As well, he outlines a recipe for *Svogliata*, which is a pie made in exactly the same manner as *Torta Pasqualina* but is filled with sliced apples and candied fruit, rather like an apfelstrudel. His *Torte di Spinaci*, spinach tart, is made in the following manner.

> To make a Spinach Tart: One takes the spinach, cleans it then puts it to wilt in a pot or pan, when it is wilted one squeezes it, adds salt and pepper, lemon peel finely pared, a couple of anchovies well chopped, raisins and pine kernels and this will serve for the filling of a *torta magra* [a fast day dish].

Another recipe for spinach *barchiglie*, boat-shaped canapés, includes *prosciutto*, soft cheese and chicken livers. The *torta* and the *barchiglie* were made with *pasta frolla*, a version of fleur pastry.

> To make *pasta frolla*: To make a tart, for every six people one takes two pounds of flour, one and a half pounds of butter, eight ounces of sugar, three egg yolks, a little white wine and a little salt. Then one combines everything together into a paste. In proportion to the number of people one increases or decreases the amounts. This pastry will serve for *torte, barchiglie, castagnette, pasticetti.*

Santi Puppo's fleur pastry must have been very rich with its high proportion of butter. Interestingly, he uses wine instead of lemon juice to make the pastry crisp.

Torta Pasqualina
Genoese Easter Pie

filo or flaky
   pastry
spinach
cream cheese
curd or ricotta
   cheese
eggs
parmesan
marjoram
butter
olive oil

To mix and roll a fine enough pastry to make a genuine *Torta Pasqualina* requires a great deal of time which perhaps not everyone would want to devote to the task, but a good result can be obtained by using filo pastry bought at a Greek food store. Lacking this, a flaky pastry will also make a delicious pie.

To line a round sloping-sided pie dish 8½ inches by 2 inches you will need 8 oz/220 g packet of filo pastry containing at least 12 sheets, or about 14 oz/400 g of flaky pastry, and olive oil as needed. For the filling you will need 14 oz/2½ cups/400 g of cooked well-drained and finely chopped fresh spinach or beet greens (5 lb/2 kg of fresh spinach will give you 1 lb/450 g cooked – and will have a more satisfactory texture than frozen spinach). Then, 3 tablespoons of freshly grated parmesan cheese; salt and pepper; 6 or 7 fresh sweet marjoram leaves; 7 oz/¾ cup/200 g of cream cheese; 7 oz/¾ cup/200 g curd cheese or drained ricotta; 4 hazelnut-sized lumps of butter; 4 very fresh eggs. Oven temperature: 400°F/200°C/6.

Oil the tin lightly with a good light olive oil, preferably from the Ponentine coast of Liguria. Lay on the first sheet of filo, pressing it closely to the sides of the tin. Leave the overlapping edges as they are. With a brush cover the pastry with a thin slick of the oil. Next add another sheet of filo, this time applying it at a slight angle to the first so that the spare edges will fan out like the petals of a sunflower. Otherwise you will end up with thick flaps of pastry on two sides of the dish and nothing on the others. Continue this process, oiling each sheet as you go until you have applied six of them. Reserve the other six under a damp teacloth for the lid of the pie. If using flaky pastry, line the oiled tin with one piece and reserve another for the lid.

Take the lined pie dish and in it spread in an even layer the well-drained and squeezed spinach. Sprinkle on two tablespoons of the grated parmesan and a little salt and pepper, and arrange the marjoram leaves here and there. Next mix the cream cheese with the curd cheese or ricotta and spread it on top of the spinach. Make four impressions with a spoon and into them place the nuts of butter. Crack one egg into each dent, then sprinkle on more salt and pepper and the rest of the parmesan. The filling should come level with the rim of the dish.

Now take the rest of the sheets of filo and lay them one atop the other over the pie, angling them exactly as you did for the bottom layers and remembering to oil each one until the six are used up. Take the overlapping pastry, cut off the points and then roll it up and around towards the centre of the pie, making a twisted cord like the folds of a turban all around the edge of the pie. Use a little oil to secure the roll, and more to moisten the entire surface of the *torta*. Pierce the top of the pastry here and there, being careful not to break the egg yolks. If using flaky pastry simply cover the pie with a sheet of pastry, trim and seal the edges, and pierce the surface here and there with a sharp fork.

Cook the *torta* in a preheated oven for about thirty-five to forty minutes.

Serve without any additions except for a glass of cold white wine. As in Angelo Guerra's ravioli (see page 145), the marjoram, isolated by creamy cheese and spinach, will provide a pleasant surprise.

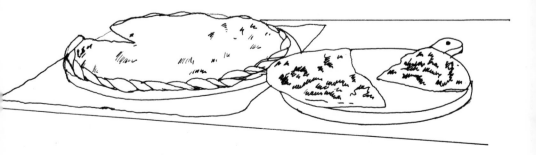

Torta di Funghi
Genoese Mushroom Pie

filo or flaky
pastry
ovoli or morels
(or field
mushrooms
and porcini)
cream cheese
curd or ricotta
cheese
parmesan
garlic
oregano
marjoram
olive oil

This pie is like the *Torta Pasqualina* (see previous recipe) but instead of the layer of chopped greens uses the following mushroom mixture. The eggs are omitted, which is customary when the pie contains ingredients other than green-leaved vegetables. For a really superb flavour this filling should be made with *ovoli* (*amanita caesarea*) or *morel* mushrooms. In the absence of these use large cultivated or field mushrooms and an ounce or so of dried *porcini* to enrich the flavour.

You will need 8 oz/220 g of filo pastry (about 12 sheets) or 14 oz/400 g of flaky pastry, and olive oil as needed. For the filling you will need 2 tablespoons of olive oil; 1 clove of garlic cut into slivers; 1 lb/450 g of fresh mushrooms, cleaned, trimmed and sliced, plus 2 oz/1 cup/50 g of dried porcini *if perforce they are necessary, which you must first soak in hot water for 10 minutes, squeeze dry and chop finely; salt and pepper; ½ teaspoon of dried oregano (see note on page 37); 3 tablespoons of freshly grated parmesan cheese; 6 or 7 fresh sweet marjoram leaves; 7 oz/¾ cup/200 g of cream cheese; 7 oz/¾ cup/200 g of curd cheese or drained ricotta. Oven temperatue: 400°F/200°C/6.*

Fill an eight and a half inch by two inch pie dish with the pastry as described in the previous recipe. Then, in a sauté pan heat the olive oil and allow the garlic to hiss in it, but do not brown as this would only serve to make it bitter. Add the sliced mushrooms and if necessary the plumped-up dried *funghi*. Turn them in the oil, lower the heat and allow the mushrooms to give up their juice. Sprinkle on a little salt and pepper, and the oregano. When the mushrooms are soft, take them from the heat and let them cool completely. If there remains a great deal of liquid in the pan, drain it off and use it in a soup or sauce.

Take the lined pie dish and in it spread the mushroom mixture in an even layer. Sprinkle on salt and pepper, two tablespoons of the grated parmesan, and arrange the marjoram leaves here and there. Next mix the cream cheese with the curd or ricotta cheese and spread it on top of the mushrooms. Sprinkle on the remaining parmesan. The filling should come level with the rim of the dish.

Now take the rest of the sheets of filo and lay them one atop the other over the pie, angling them as with the bottom layers and oiling each one until the six are used up. Take the overlapping pastry, cut off the points and then roll it up and around towards the centre of the pie, making a twisted cord like the folds of a turban all around the edge of the pie. Use a little oil to secure the roll, and more to moisten the entire surface of the *torta*. Pierce the top of the pie here and there. If using flaky pastry, simply cover the pie with a sheet of pastry, trim and seal the edges, and pierce with a fork.

Cook the *torta* in a preheated oven for about thirty-five to forty minutes.

Torta di Carciofi
Artichoke Pie

Torta Pasqualina (see page 148) becomes *Torta di Carciofi* when you use artichokes instead of green-leaved vegetables as the first layer of filling.

You will need 8 oz/220 g of filo pastry (12 sheets) or 14 oz/400 g of flaky pastry, and olive oil as needed. For the filling you will need about 18 fresh or frozen artichoke hearts; juice of 1 lemon; 1 small onion; 5 sprigs of parsley; 1 tablespoon of olive oil; 1 tablespoon or more of butter; salt and freshly milled black pepper; 3 tablespoons of freshly grated parmesan cheese; 6 or 7 sweet marjoram leaves; 7 oz/³/₄ cup/200 g of cream cheese; 7 oz/³/₄ cup/200 g of curd cheese or drained ricotta. Oven temperature: 400°F/200°C/6.

filo or flaky
    pastry
artichoke hearts
cream cheese
curd or ricotta
    cheese
onion
parmesan
lemon juice
parsley
marjoram
butter
olive oil

Line an eight and a half inch by two inch pie dish with the pastry as described on page 148. Then, trim and slice the artichokes vertically from tip to stem, and plunge them into cold water to which you have added the lemon juice to prevent them from blackening. Chop the onion and parsley together finely. Heat the oil and butter in a large sauté pan and add the onion and parsley; allow the onion to become transparent but do not allow it to brown. Dry the artichoke slices and add them to the pan; turn them and let them cook without browning until they are nearly tender, seasoning them with salt and pepper. Add more butter if the mixture becomes dry. Let the mixture cool completely before adding to the *Torta*.

Take the lined pie dish and spread in the artichoke mixture evenly. Season, sprinkle on two tablespoons of the parmesan, and scatter the marjoram leaves here and there. Mix the soft cheeses together and spread them on top, then add the remaining parmesan.

Lay the remaining sheets of filo over the top of the pie, oiling them as you go. Take the overlapping pastry, trim the points, and then roll it up and around towards the centre of the pie, making a twisted cord like the folds of a turban around the edge. Use a little oil to secure the roll and more to moisten the entire surface. Pierce the top of the pie here and there. If using flaky pastry, simply cover the pie with a sheet, trim and seal the edges, and pierce with a fork. Cook the *Torta* in a preheated oven for about thirty-five to forty minutes.

TORTE VARIE
PIES FROM LIGURIA
AND OTHER REGIONS

Torta d'Erbe
Green Pie

fleur pastry
spinach
leeks or onion
ricotta cheese
parmesan
eggs
borage
butter or olive
   oil

Torta d'Erbe has been made in Italy for hundreds of years. It usually contains green leaves of diverse varieties like beet greens, swiss chard or spinach, borage or sorrel, fat cheeses like *ravigiolo* or ricotta, and is enlivened by spices like nutmeg and cinnamon. Very often small quantities of *prosciutto*, fresh sausage or *salame* are mixed in to add to the savour. Originally sweet ingredients like sugar, pine kernels and sultanas were included but today the taste for such mixtures, outside oriental cooking, has all but disappeared.

Torta d'Erbe was made under many different names. Christofaro di Messisbugo in his *Libro Novo* published in Venice in 1567 calls his '*Torta d'Erbe alla Ferrarese o Romagnnola*' and in it he put a *chiffonade* of beet greens, herbs, fat cheese, milk and butter, and half-way through the baking he sprinkled four ounces of sugar on top of the crust.

You will need fleur pastry made with 5½ oz/1½ cups/150 g of flour (see page 155); 2 lb/1 kg of fresh young spinach or beet greens (to make about 7 oz/1 cup/200 g cooked weight); a few sprigs of borage; salt; 2 small leeks or 1 medium-size sweet onion; 2 tablespoons butter or olive oil; 7oz/¾ cup/200 g of ricotta cheese; 3 tablespoons of freshly grated parmesan cheese; 2 beaten eggs; freshly milled black pepper; egg yolk for gilding the pastry. Oven temperature: 375°F/190°C/5.

Wash the green leaves and the borage, remove the thick stems and roll the greenery into bundles which you must then cut into a fine chiffonade with a sharp knife. As you cut the tiny strips lay them in a bowl and sprinkle them lightly with salt. Put them aside for their liquid to drain away. You may alternatively blanch, drain and then chop the greenery.

Clean and finely chop the leeks or onion. Melt the butter or warm the oil in a pan, add the leeks or onion and let them become transparent but do not even allow them to become blonde, let alone brown. Set aside to cool. Rinse the greenery to free it of salt and pat it dry with a clean cloth or kitchen paper. When the leeks or onion are cool add them to the greenery in a large bowl. In another bowl mix the ricotta, parmesan and beaten eggs and season this well with salt and black pepper. Combine this soft paste with the greenery and mix it evenly.

Tip the filling into the lined tart tin and smooth down the surface. Use the scraps of dough to make a decorative lattice. Gild the pastry with an egg yolk and bake the pie in a preheated oven for thirty-five minutes.

You may also bake this filling in a covered pie using a normal short-crust pastry, which is easier to handle and more suitable for covered pies. Italians, however, use *pasta frolla* a great deal and very often mould the pastry with their fingertips to fill the tin properly after rolling it out roughly. They push the dough into place at the edges of the tin as they do when making a tray of pizza with leavened bread dough.

Either version of the pie is delicious as a first course to a dinner or as a luncheon dish served perhaps with *peperoni*, red bell peppers grilled then marinated in excellent olive oil.

Torta d'Erbe Condita *Spiced Green Pie*

To make a more robust version of *Torta d'Erbe*, add the following ingredients to the previous recipe: five or six fresh basil leaves sweated with the leeks or onion; a sprinkling of cayenne pepper and 2 oz/50 g of finely diced fried *pancetta* or bacon added to the filling.

Torta del Venerdì Santo
Good Friday Pie

This is a southern Italian recipe for a *magra*, a meatless dish to be eaten on Good Friday or other fast days. It contains nothing but vegetables and anchovies.

For the dough you will need 10½ oz/3 cups/300 g of plain or American all-purpose flour; ½ teaspoon salt; ¼ pint/scarce ¾ cup/150 ml of olive oil; 1 egg; water as needed. For the filling you will need 2 lb/1 kg of a mixture of fennel, onion, beet greens and red bell peppers; 3 tablespoons of olive oil; 6 anchovy fillets; 1 oz/25 g of pitted black olives; ½ oz/15 g of capers; salt and black pepper. Oven temperature: 400°F/200°C/6.

fennel
onion
beet greens
red bell pepper
anchovies
black olives
capers
flour
egg
olive oil

Knead the flour, olive oil, egg and a little water together to form a smooth dough, then put it aside in a bowl in a cool place, covered with a cloth, for thirty minutes.

Chop the cleaned and trimmed vegetables into small pieces and blanch them for a few minutes in boiling salted water. Drain them well, squeezing out excess water. In a sauté or frying pan heat the olive oil then add the vegetables and let them soften but not lose all of their crispness. Allow the vegetables to cool completely then in a bowl mix with the anchovy fillets, broken in pieces, the olives and the capers. Season with salt and abundant black pepper, but be sparing with the salt as the anchovies will provide their own.

Knead the dough again briefly, then cut it into two pieces and roll each one out thinly. Line a greased shallow nine inch tart tin with one sheet of dough. On this spread out the filling and cover it with the second sheet of dough. Seal and primp the edges and pierce the surface of the pie here and there with the tines of a fork. Bake in a pre-heated oven for about twenty-five to thirty minutes until the pastry is golden.

This is a severe but savoury pie and is good when served with a fresh sharp tomato sauce (see page 52) or slices of ripe tomato laid at the last minute on top of the crust before it is brought to the table. A trickle of spiced olive oil in which a red chilli pepper has been marinated is also a good addition.

Torta di Funghi
Mushroom Tart

fleur pastry
pancetta
porcini
parsley
eggs
parmesan
cream
garlic
olive oil

This is an elegant mushroom tart properly made with fresh *porcini* gathered from Tuscan woods, whose rich velvety taste contrasts well with a crisp buttery pastry.

You will need fleur pastry made with 5½ oz/1½ cups/150 g of flour (see opposite); 2 tablespoons of olive oil; 1 finely sliced clove of garlic; 2 oz/½ cup/50 g of diced pancetta; *9 oz/250 g of* porcini *or field mushrooms, cleaned and sliced; 1 tablespoon of finely chopped parsley; salt and pepper; 3 eggs; 2 oz/¾ cup/50 g of freshly grated parmesan cheese; a spoonful or two of thin cream if required. Oven temperature: 375°F/190°C/5.*

In a large sauté or frying pan heat the olive oil and garlic, add the diced *pancetta* and allow it to change colour but not to burn. Then add the mushrooms and turn them in the oil; let them cook fairly briskly, shaking the pan to make sure they do not catch and burn. Add the parsley and a little salt and pepper. When the mushrooms are cooked take the pan from the heat and let the mixture cool completely.

Line a greased nine to ten inch shallow tart tin with the pastry and trim the edges neatly. In a bowl mix the eggs with the parmesan cheese, season lightly then add the cooled mushrooms and mix everything together evenly. If the mixture is very dry add a spoonful or so of cream. Tip the mixture into the tart tin and bake it in a preheated oven until the pastry is golden and the eggs just set, about thirty-five minutes. If you bake in a proved dark tin and put the tin on a metal plaque which has been heating in the oven, the bottom of the pastry will brown more satisfactorily. You may also serve this mushroom mixture in individual tartlets.

If fortune presents you with *porcini* this makes an excellent first course to a dinner party served with a white wine of character that has not been over-iced. To enliven cultivated mushrooms mix them with a few dried *porcini* that you have plumped up in hot water.

Pasta Frolla *Fleur Pastry*

You will need for the pastry 5½ oz/1½ cups/150 g of plain cake flour; 1 teaspoon of salt; 2½ oz/ a generous ½ stick/60 g of butter; 1 egg yolk; ½ teaspoon of lemon juice; a little iced water as needed.

Sift the flour and salt into a bowl. Cut the butter into small pieces and rub or cut into the flour, until you are left with a mixture the texture of breadcrumbs. Add the beaten egg, lemon juice and a few drops of water, bringing the mixture together with a fork into a dough. Knead this as briefly and as lightly as possible. Cover and leave in a cool place for at least an hour. Fleur pastry can be difficult to handle – if it breaks, press it into shape in the tin with your fingertips.

Crostata di Fegatini
Chicken Liver Tart

You will need fleur pastry made with 5½ oz/1½ cups/150 g flour as given in the recipe above; 1 tablespoon of olive oil; 4 oz/1 cup/100 g of diced pancetta; *10 oz/1½ cups/300 g of chicken livers; 3 tablespoons of dry vin santo or dry sherry; 3 eggs; 2 tablespoons of fine home-made breadcrumbs; 2 oz/½ cup/50 g of freshly grated parmesan cheese. Oven temperature: 375°F/190°C/5.*

fleur pastry
pancetta
chicken livers
vin santo or dry sherry
breadcrumbs
parmesan
eggs
olive oil

Heat the olive oil in a sauté pan, add the diced *pancetta* and let it change colour but not become too brown, then add the whole chicken livers, making sure that they are well-cleaned and without the slightest trace of green bile which would ruin the dish with its extreme bitterness. Cook the livers for a few minutes until they are set then add the vin santo and let it evaporate. Take the pan from the heat, allow the contents to cool then chop them, but not so finely as to make a paste.

Next, in a bowl, mix the eggs with the breadcrumbs and the parmesan. To this add the chopped liver mixture and combine the two together. Line a nine to ten inch tart tin with the pastry, spoon in the filling and bake the tart in a preheated oven for about thirty minutes until the crust is golden and the eggs set.

This tart is good hot or cold; when hot it makes a good supper or luncheon dish and when cold, cut into thin slices, it forms an interesting part of a mixed antipasto, perhaps with *barchette con crema di funghi tartufati*, which are tiny oval pastry cases filled with mushroom-flavoured béchamel and topped with a slice of black truffle.

Torta di Cipolle ed Acciughe
Onion and Anchovy Pie

onions
parsley
nutmeg
anchovies
flour
butter
egg yolk

For the pasta brisée *(shortcrust pastry) you will need 8 oz/2 cups/240 g of plain or American all-purpose flour; ½ teaspoon salt; 2 oz/½ stick/50 g of butter; a little iced water; 1 egg yolk to gild the pastry. For the filling you need 4 white onions; 2 tablespoons of butter; salt and freshly milled black pepper; nutmeg; 2 tablespoons of finely chopped parsley; 4 or 5 anchovy fillets. Oven temperature: 400°F/200°C/6.*

In a pastry bowl add the salt to the sifted flour. Cut the butter into the flour with a knife or pastry cutter, until it has the texture of fine bread-crumbs. Add a little iced water and mix into a dough, handling as briefly and lightly as possible. Put aside in a cool place for at least thirty minutes.

Slice the onions into fine rings and soften them in a sauté pan with the butter; keep the heat very low and do not allow the onions to colour, merely to wilt. Season them with a little salt, black pepper and freshly grated nutmeg. Add the chopped parsley, mix it in, and let the mixture cool completely.

Divide the pastry into two pieces, one a little larger than the other. Roll out the big half into a circle and with it line a greased nine to ten inch shallow tart tin. Roll out the second smaller piece to form the pie's crust. Tip the onion mixture into the lined tin and spread them evenly. Break the anchovies into pieces and scatter them over the onions. Put on the top layer of pastry, trim, seal and primp the edges. Pierce the surface here and there with the tines of a fork, and, finally, gild the top with a beaten egg yolk applied with a pastry brush.

Bake the *torta* in a preheated oven until the pastry is golden, about thirty minutes.

This Tuscan onion tart is good with a rocket salad or *fagioli verdi lessati*, boiled green beans served warm with a seasoning of the best Tuscan olive oil, a little salt, and abundant black pepper.

SELECT BIBLIOGRAPHY

Athenaeus, *The Deipnosophists* (trans. Gulick C. B., London, 1969-71)

Brighigna A., *Le Olive da Tavola* (Bologna, 1984)

de Bourcard Francesco, *Usi e Costumi di Napoli* (Naples 1857-1866)

Cato, *De Re Rustica* (trans. Hooper W. D., Ash H. B., London, 1979)

Columella, *De Re Rustica*, I-IV (trans. Ash H. B., London, 1979)

Corrado Vincenzo, *Il Cuoco Galante* (Naples, 1773)

Darby W. J., Ghalioungui P., Grivetti L., *Food: The Gift of Osiris* (New York, 1977)

David E., *English Bread and Yeast Cookery* (Harmondsworth, 1979)

Davidson A., *Mediterranean Seafood* (2nd ed., London, 1981)

Dosi A., Schell F., *A Tavola con I Romani Antichi* (Bologna, 1984)

Encyclopaedia Judaica (Jerusalem, 1972)

Food and Wine: The Guide to Good Taste, vol. 8, no. 7 (New York, 1985)

Francesconi J. C., *La Cucina Napoletana* (Naples, 1985)

Goethe J. W., *Italian Journey* (trans. Auden W. H., Mayer E., London, 1970)

Hitti P. K., *History of the Arabs* (London, 1943)

Kenyon K. M., *Archaeology in the Holy Land* (4th ed., London, 1979)

Lexikon Der Ägyptologie, ed., Helck W., Otto E. (Weisbaden, 1975)

Messisbugo Christofaro, *Libro Novo* (Venice, 1557)

Origo I., *The Merchant of Prato* (London, 1963)

Porcaro G., *Sapore di Napoli* (Naples, 1985)

Romer E., *The Tuscan Year* (London, 1984)

Rosellini H., *I Monumenti dell'Egitto e della Nubia*, Vol. II, 'Monumenti Civili' (Pisa, 1834)

Rossi A., *I Formaggi* (Milan, 1985)

Rossi E., *La Vera Cuciniera Genovese* (Milan, 1973)

Santi Puppo P., *Il Cuciniere Moderno* (circ. 1780)

Tanara Vincenzo, *L'Economia del Cittadino in Villa* (Bologna, 1644)

Varro, *De Re Rustica* (trans. Hooper W. D., Ash H. B., London, 1979)

Willensky, Elliot, *When Brooklyn was the World 1920-1957* (New York, 1986)

Grateful acknowledgment is made to the following sources:

De re Rustica, Cato translated by W. D. Hooper and H. B. Ash. Heinemann London, 1979.

Food and Wine Magazine Stanley Dry Restaurant Column. Reprinted by permission from the July, 1985 issue of Food and Wine. Copyright 1985 The International Review of Food and Wine Associates.

Italian Journey by Johann Goethe, translated by W. H. Auden and Elizabeth Mayer. Collins Publishers, London.

Sapori di Napoli, Guiseppe Porcaro 1985, Adriano Gallina, Editore, Naples.

The Merchant of Prato by Iris Origo. Peregrine Books (Penguin). London 1963.

The Tuscan Year, Elizabeth Romer. Weidenfeld (Publishers) Limited, 1984.

When Brooklyn Was The World 1920-57, Elliot Willensky. Harmony Books.

INDEX